# ART AND ARCHAEOLOGY OF SOUTH-EAST ASIA

— Recent Perspectives —

# ART AND ARCHAEOLOGY OF SOUTH-EAST ASIA

## — Recent Perspectives —

Edited by

Bachchan Kumar

Indira Gandhi National Centre for the Arts
New Delhi

Aryan Books International
New Delhi

ART AND ARCHAEOLOGY OF SOUTH-EAST ASIA

ISBN: 978-81-7305-408-2



Published in **2011** by :

**INDIRA GANDHI NATIONAL CENTRE FOR THE ARTS**
Central Vista Mess, Janpath, New Delhi-110001 (India)

and

**ARYAN BOOKS INTERNATIONAL**
Pooja Apartments, 4B, Ansari Road, New Delhi-110002 (India)
Tel.: 23287589, 23255799; Fax: 91-11-23270385
E-mail: aryanbooks@vsnl.com, aryanbooks@gmail.com
**www.aryanbooks.co.in**

Computer Typeset and Printed in India at
ABI Prints & Publishing Co., New Delhi

# Preface

Sir John Marshall writes "To know Indian art in India alone is to know only half story." This statement has been further elaborated by French savant Sylvain Lévi – "India produced her ultimate master-pieces only through foreign influence and in foreign lands." It appears true through the study of painstaking scholars. The archaeological remains of culture and civilisation and the extraordinary creativity and brilliance of traditional art and architecture that flourished in South-East Asia, especially in the mainland region, make this area most exciting. Unfortunately this area has been insufficiently explored and rather neglected. Keeping this in view, the Indira Gandhi National Centre for the Arts organized two successive Seminars on the themes – "The Art of Vietnam and Cambodia" and "The Art of Laos" on November 8, 1995 and August 12, 1997 respectively. The present volume is based on the papers presented in these Seminars.

The first paper "Archaeology of Mainland South-East Asia and its Implications for Art History," presented by Himanshu Prabha Ray, stresses the need of formulating the research strategy for the study of ancient architectural remains, especially temples and monastic establishments in their social and religious context. The drawback in the existing framework is that it makes use of only archaeological data in conjunction with inscriptions and other literary texts whereas it does not take into consideration the socio-cultural context. It is argued that cultural contact between South and South-East Asia started several centuries prior to the appearance of the earliest inscriptions and temples in the 4th-5th centuries AD. The nature of the long contacts needs to be examined by analysing archaeological data to understand the gradual social changes, which led to the emergence of temple architecture and got reflected in the variations in their styles and functions. Drawing our attention to the existing drawback, Ray has tried to present a tentative research framework, which needs to be examined with reference to the primary data.

In the next paper "Prehistoric Art to Folk Art: A Possible Continuity in South-East Asia", D.K. Bhattacharya discusses the progression of ethnic Indian art in South-East Asia. The Indian contact with South-East Asia, he suggests, can be traced back to pre-historic period. Early contact between Bihar, Bengal and Northeast India and South-East Asia can be established with occurrence of shouldered celts in both the regions during Neolithic and later periods. This paper also reveals the similarity of the decoration pattern of the ceramics excavated from the Gulf of Siam belonging to the period between 500 BC and AD 900 with *Kohbar* (ethnic art) decoration pattern of Chotanagpur area of Bihar (India).

The kingdom of Champa, whose inhabitants spoke languages of Indonesian linguistic group, came into existence at the end of the 2nd century AD near central part of Vietnam. The oldest Sanskrit inscription belonging to the period of 3rd or 4th century AD mentions about a king who claims his lineage from the family of Śrī-Māra. The third paper written by M.N. Deshpande is a slightly amended version of his paper published in the Vivekananda Commemoration Volume in 1970. In this paper he presents an appraisal of various schools of the art style of Champa and links it with the styles of India. Basing his arguments on the epigraphical, archaeological and architectural evidences, relating to Śaivism, Vaiṣṇavism and Buddhism, he expresses the opinion that "Champa was an outpost of Indian Culture."

J.C. Sharma brings to light architectural development of the temples of Champa during different periods. He has classified the development of temple architecture into four stages. The advanced stage has been considered between AD 982 to 1471. At that period, Hindu temples were constructed based on Indian design. The native characters of the Mi-son temples were replaced by refinement and delicateness of Indian temples. The Javanese architectural beauty can also be seen at this stage of development. The sculptural works including carvings and decorations on outer walls, copulas, pillars and pilasters have also been discussed.

The most developed Cham art style known as Dong-duong art which flourished in the present Quang-nam Danang area of Vietnam during the later part of 9th century, had Mahayanist imprint. The fifth paper "The Dong-duong Art of Vietnam" presented by Bachchan Kumar examines architecture and art styles of Dong-duong and links it with Indian and neighbouring art styles. The architectural styles of the important Buddhist temples of Dong-duong including a temple dedicated to Lakṣmīndralokeśvara were based on the layout of Paharpur (U.P., India) brick temple. The sculptures show a fairly developed art style based on indigenous traditional art. The floral decoration enhances the beauty of the art in that period. It was a golden period of Cham art and royal patronage played a significant role in its development.

In the next paper Prof. Lokesh Chandra presents an overview of the art of Vietnam and Cambodia. Both Vietnam and Cambodia have distinct cultural identity. Ancient Culture of Vietnam revolves around the coastal Indo-China. The Chams under the kingdom of Champa governed this area. Its first dynasty was of Indian origin. Vietnamese art predominantly shows Chinese influence with tenets of Buddhism. Cambodia has been a centre of attraction since Henri Mouhot brought to light the ruins of Angkor in 1860. The monuments of Angkor reveal mass impact of Gāndhāra art style. Prof. Chandra classifies the Cambodian art and precisely discusses its salient features.

The gorgeous Vaiṣṇavite temple Angkor Wat, built by Sūryavarman II, depicts a variety of fine decorative reliefs in the form of humans, flowers, and animals. K.M. Srivastava in his paper entitled "Apsarās at Angkor Wat" mentions various *apsarās* depicted on the walls of Angkor Wat. The *apsarās,* shown both in single and in group of two to six, delineate an art style developed indigenously. Contrary to *apsarās* in Indian art, the Ankorian *apsarās* are not heavily ornamented. The headdresses are of various kinds. The expression of feminine beauty reveals serenity in Cambodian art.

Ethnically, Laotians are related to the Tais. They practise Hīnayāna form of Buddhism. Various elements from the Rāmāyaṇa are embedded in their performing art. A.K. Das's paper "Lao Tai Muang and Art Manifestation" examines some art forms of Lao Tai, which have similarities with the people of North-East India. The Tais of North-East India still maintain their cultural identity by practising some unique art forms though they have assimilated local culture. The Assamese women's skirt (*mekhlā*) with *butadiya* pattern, shoulder cloth (*reha*) with *kesh basa* technique and *gamucha* (towel) with typical *fulam* pattern of red weft supplementary technique are the tradition of the Tais. The Assamese *bihuwan* has much similarity with *phachet,* a shoulder cloth woven as love gift for a man in Laos.

The ninth paper "Buddhist art of Laos" presented by Bachchan Kumar consists of four parts. From first to third part, it discusses the origin of the people of Laos, foundation of the Laotian kingdom and rise of Buddhism in Laos respectively. The Buddhist art of Laos has been analysed in the fourth part, which discusses the art and architecture. The sculptures of Laos primarily bear the imprint of Mon-Khmer art of Dvārāvatī period. The Laotian art, in the later stage of development, imbibed the characteristic features of various schools of Thai art based on Indian art styles of Gupta and post-Gupta period. This paper also examines the architectural pattern of the Laotian *vihāras* (monasteries), *stūpas*, pagodas as well as decorative patterns and paintings on these religious monuments.

The Rāmāyaṇa is deeply rooted in the Laotian culture. A number of Rāma stories is prevalent in Laos. The Buddhist monks recite it as part of their folklore. Its artistic manifestations are found in the Buddhist monasteries and other temples. In the tenth paper, Induja Awasthi briefly appraises the depiction of the Rāmāyaṇa in different art forms in the temples of Laos. The Rāmāyaṇa is also present in the mural paintings of Vat Oup Moung in Vientiane and other temples of Laos. She also discusses in brief the bearing of the Rāmāyaṇa on performing art of Laos.

The last paper "The Mural Paintings of Laos" written by Neeru Misra traces briefly religious impact on the Laotian paintings. The Laotian culture has a blend of both the religions, i.e. Hinduism and Theravada form of Buddhism. That is why the Laotian paintings are based on religious themes. The scenes from Laotian versions of the Rāmāyaṇa and previous life of Buddha narrated in *Jātakas* are depicted on the mural paintings of the temples. She also discusses in brief the technique of Laotian painting, which is greatly influenced by Thai art.

## ACKNOWLEDGEMENTS

These two seminars were possible only through the direction of Dr. Kapila Vatsyayan, the then Academic Director and former President of the Indira Gandhi National Centre for the Arts Trust, New Delhi. Prof. N.R. Shetty, the then Member Secretary, IGNCA made the publication of the Seminar papers possible. I am deeply beholden to Dr. K.K. Chakravarty, former Member Secretary, IGNCA and Dr. Jyotindra Jain, Member Secretary, IGNCA for giving all support in bringing out this publication. I sincerely thank Prof. Gaya Charan Tripathi, Head of the Department of Kala Kosa, IGNCA for encouraging me to bring out this publication. I express my deep sense of gratitude to all the contributors of the paper. My thanks are due to all library staff of IGNCA for providing me ready reference and other such allied assistance. Finally I thank Shri Vikas Arya, Aryan Books International, New Delhi for this extraordinary publication.

**Bachchan Kumar**
(Editor)

# Contents

# Abbreviations

| | | |
|---|---|---|
| *AA* | : | *Arts Asiatiques*, Paris |
| *AP* | : | *Asian Perspectives: The Journal of Archaeology for Asia and the Pacific*, Honolulu, USA |
| *BARL* | : | *Bulletin des Amis du Royaume Lao* |
| *BAVH* | : | *Bulletin des Amis du Vieux Hue*, Vietnam |
| *BCAI* | : | *Bulletin de la Commission Archéologique de l'Indochinoise*, Paris |
| *BEFEO* | : | *Bulletin de l'École Française d'Extrême-Orient*, Paris |
| *BKI* | : | *Bijdragen tot de Taal-, Land-en Volkenkunde* published by the Koninklijk Instituut voor Taal-, Land-en Volkenkunde, Leiden |
| *BMFEA* | : | *Bulletin of the Museum of Far Eastern Antiquities*, Stockholm, Sweden |
| *EFEO* | : | *L'École Française d'Extrême-Orient*, Paris |
| *INTACH* | : | Indian National Trust for Art and Cultural Heritage |
| *IMB* | : | *Indian Museum Bulletin*, Calcutta |
| *IAR* | : | *Indian Archaeology—A Review*, New Delhi |
| *JA* | : | *Journal Asiatique*, Paris |
| *JAS* | : | *Journal of the Asiatic Society*, Calcutta |
| *JBORS* | : | *Journal of the Bihar and Orissa Research Society*, Bankipore, Patna, Bihar |
| *JGIS* | : | *Journal of the Greater India Society*, Calcutta |
| *JHKAS* | : | *Journal of the Hong Kong Archaeological Society*, Hong Kong |
| *JOR* | : | *Journal of Oriental Research*, Madras |
| *JRAS* | : | *Journal of the Royal Asiatic Society of Great Britain and Ireland*, London |
| *JSS* | : | *Journal of the Siam Society*, Bangkok |
| *JUP* | : | *Journal of the University of Poona*, Pune |

| | | |
|---|---|---|
| *MQRSEA* | : | *Modern Quaternary Research in Southeast Asia* |
| *NG* | : | *National Geographic*, Washington, D.C. |
| *VSS* | : | *Vietnam Social Sciences*, Hanoi, Vietnam |

# List of Illustrations

# 1

# The Archaeology of Mainland South-East Asia and Its Implications for Art History

Himanshu Prabha Ray

This paper is really an attempt at formulating a research strategy for the study of ancient architectural remains, especially temples and monastic establishments in their social and religious context in South-East Asia. Even in South Asia, this continues to be a largely neglected topic, though there has been some work on the economic networks of the South Indian temple complexes. The framework presented here remains somewhat tentative as it needs to be validated with reference to primary data from Vietnam and Cambodia, as my own fieldwork has hitherto been largely in peninsular South-East Asia and the Indonesian archipelago.

It was around the middle of the first millennium AD that inscriptions in Sanskrit first appeared in mainland and peninsular South-East Asia. These record the genealogies of early rulers in the region, who often trace their ancestry to Indian princes and merchants. The traditional chronicles of Burma, for example, narrate that the earliest kingdom in the Irrawaddy Valley was founded by a prince who came from India, having lost his land there. Similarly, the introduction of Indian culture to Cambodia is attributed to the Brahmin Kauṇḍinya who married a Cambodian princess. It is also to the 4th-5th centuries AD that sculptural and architectural representations in the Buddhist and Brahmanical idiom date. These manifestations, when coupled with references to Suvarṇabhūmi in early Sanskrit and Pāli literature have led scholars to attribute social change in South-East Asia to external influences, viz., Indian and Chinese. In the words of Coedés:[1] "It is interesting to note that even in prehistoric times the autochthonous peoples of Indo-China seem to have been lacking in creative genius and showed little aptitude for making progress without stimulus from outside."

This point of view may perhaps be countered with a quote from De Casparis[2] who pointed out in 1983 that it is not the "intention to demolish existing theories about 'Indianisation' but rather to call attention to some of their weaknesses and so to prepare the way for a more satisfactory approach" thus substituting it by "a lasting relationship between the Indian subcontinent and maritime South-East Asia. The relatively simple, or perhaps simplistic, view of Indianisation is replaced by a complicated network of relations, both between various parts of each of the two great regions and between the two regions themselves".[3]

A second factor that should be taken cognizance of is the passive role that has so far been attributed to religious tradition both in archaeological and historical writing from the subcontinent. Religion has been seen as providing legitimacy to the emerging ruling elite or as an agent of integration by appropriating and absorbing local cults. These issues have been discussed largely in the context of Brahmanism and studies on Buddhism and Jainism have been few and far between. This is amply reflected in current debates in South-East Asian historiography where the discussion has centred around the presence of Brahmanas as indicated by several early inscriptions especially those from Vo-canh and Kutei and it has been argued that "Brahmins appear to have been invited particularly as a sort of 'extra' legitimators for a new and more advanced type of authority which was not sanctioned by the traditional societies of South-East Asia".[4] Similarly, the study of architectural and sculptural remains has largely focused on the development of styles and similarities and influences between the different regions. There are very few works[5] that have sought to integrate religious tradition within the changing belief systems of the populace or which have concentrated on the social dimensions of monumental architecture.[6] These lacunae are even more glaring in the case of South-East Asia, a region that has received scant attention either from South Asian historians or archaeologists.

These drawbacks in the existing framework may perhaps be overcome by using archaeological data in conjunction with inscriptions and literary texts. In this paper, it is argued that cultural contact between South and South-East Asia started several centuries prior to the appearance of the earliest inscriptions and temples in the 4th-5th centuries AD. The nature of this protracted contact needs to be analysed in order to comprehend the gradual changes and adaptations in the belief systems of the populace. Thus, archaeological data becomes crucial to an understanding of social change that led to the emergence of temple architecture in several regions of South-East Asia and to explain variations in styles and functions. More importantly it focuses on the need felt by the emerging political elite for endorsement from religious authority and hence patronage and support of temple and monastic construction.

Archaeological investigations during the last three decades have confirmed the indigenous beginnings of Vietnamese civilisation well before the Chinese invasions of the 1st and 2nd centuries BC. By the mid-2nd millennium BC, bronze metallurgy was well developed with bronze artefacts at one site (Dong-dau) increasing from about 20 per cent at 1400 BC to over 40 per cent at about 1100 BC. The early years of the first millennium BC saw the beginning of political centralisation and the establishment of the Van-lang kingdom. It in turn developed into the classic Dongson period, beginning somewhere between 600 and 400 BC.[7] Early writings on the Dongson culture had traced its bronze-casting technology to northern China, but this has been discredited by recent finds from north-east Thailand which indicate that bronze-casting technology developed independently in South-East Asia and that Dongson bronze technology probably developed from local or regional industries rather than from imported Chinese skills.

Crucial for our discussion is the fact that the Dongson culture is associated with a strong tradition of sailing and maritime contacts. It is characterised by bronze drums which were probably cast complete with decoration and were decorated on the sides with friezes of boats with bird-head prows and tail-feather sterns.[8] Few details of early Vietnamese water-craft can be discerned from these stylised representations, though on certain drums the portrayals are more realistic and often indicative of technological innovations, such as the drum from Ongbah cave which shows a fixed rudder suggesting deep sea navigation.[9] Similarly the depiction of sea-fish together with other members of the animal kingdom in the proximity of the ships points to their being used in the open sea.[10] The possibility of deep sea navigation by north Vietnamese communities at this time is further strengthened by the transportation of Heger I type kettledrums by sea and their extensive distribution throughout the Malay peninsula and the Sunda chain of Indonesia. They have been found all along or near the Mekong River in Laos and in central Thailand, often in association with boat burials.

Contemporary with the Dongson culture of north Vietnam was the Sa-huynh culture of the southern part of the region known primarily from jar-burial sites. The Sa-huynh sites reveal a greater usage of iron than the Dongson sites and Sa-huynh bronzes are mainly decorative items rather than tools and weapons.[11] Sa-huynh urn fields are found in coastal sand dunes and major river valleys and consist of large ovoid or cylindrical, thin-walled, lidded jars with grave goods. Contact with the bronze-working sites of the north seems to be somewhat limited as only two Heger I drums have so far been found.

Based on present evidence it would seem that around the 3rd-2nd centuries BC this regional trading system came in contact with the Indian maritime network either directly or through links with central Thailand and the Malay peninsula, leading to the import of several prestige items from the subcontinent into South-East Asia, the most commonly found at archaeological sites, especially Sa-huynh sites in Vietnam and Metal Age burial sites in mainland South-East Asia being carnelian and glass beads and sherds of knobbed and rouletted wares.[12]

There seems to have been a change both in the settlement pattern as also the maritime network around the second century AD with the emergence of the earliest urban centres in the major river valleys. Of relevance here is the site of Oc-eo in the Mekong Valley dated between the 2nd and the 7th centuries AD. It should nevertheless be stressed that Oc-eo did not arise from a void, instead the region had been settled from the late Neolithic or the early Metal Age onwards as indicated by burials found in the vicinity of the site. The ceramics from the site show similarities with those of the Sa-huynh and Dongson cultures indicating indigenous development, though the entire complex is marked by a distinctly local style.

At the same time, the site was part of a larger inland network and the material assemblage indicates similarities with that from sites in the Chao Phraya and Irrawaddy Valleys. The range of raw materials used at Oc-eo for the manufacture of jewellery was indeed extraordinary; a majority of these were imported and in addition to large quantities of gold and tin, these included diamonds, rubies, amber, garnet, jadeite, etc.[13]

Excavations by Malleret at Oc-eo yielded a variety of objects indicating the external relations of the site such as carnelian seals with Brahmi inscriptions, glass beads, statuary and Mediterranean intaglios and medallions.[14] Recent analysis shows that a distinction should perhaps be made between imports from India as contrasted to objects produced locally from Indian prototypes and those showing Indian influence adapted to local traditions.[15] Thus glass beads were initially introduced from India, but later produced locally using clay crucibles which have a long ancestry in the region. Similarly, the use of double moulds has great antiquity in South-East Asia where they were used for bronze casting. At Oc-eo these double moulds were employed in the casting of tin pendants and one of them bears a legend in a mixed Kharosthi-Brahmi script as deciphered by B.N. Mukherjee.[16]

This expansion of trading networks and emergence of urban centres in the major river valleys coincided with changes in the belief systems of early South-East Asian communities and the beginnings of brick architecture in the region. Data on this is still sparse and further research is necessary to document the shift from the early burial practices of the local communities to the acceptance of Buddhist and Brahmanical religious traditions around the middle of the first millennium AD. A number of wooden images of the Buddha have been reported from sites in the Mekong Delta radiocarbon-dated between the 2nd and 7th centuries AD,[17] together with votive and Buddhist images embossed on heavy gold foil. There are no indications of existence of any structure prior to the 5th century AD. Parmentier (1927) had suggested that the small brick sanctuaries found in the vicinity of Oc-eo may have housed wooden Buddha images found in the region, but this is an issue that needs to be resolved by further research.

Another site crucial to an understanding of the transition from prehistory to history is the site of Tra-kieu located in the Thu Bon Valley, 28 km south of Danang. French archaeologists had earlier carried out excavations at the site and had rejected any relationship between the Sa-huynh culture at the site and the emergence of the fortified settlement of Siṃhapura. Cham culture was attributed to Austronesian speaking immigrants from the Indonesian archipelago who had moved west under Indian influence. On the basis of their recent work, Vietnamese archaeologists posit a continuous evolutionary development from late Sa-huynh to Cham culture with the latter emerging around the 2nd century AD.

> The transformation of Sa-huynh to Cham was rapid and revolutionary as the small-scale chiefly village societies of the late prehistoric period were incorporated into networks of trade and exchange extending from the Mediterranean via India to China enabling village leaders to expand their spheres of influence into kingdoms supported by new forms of political and religious expression provided by India.[18]

A major factor that needs to be taken into account while explaining these shifts and changes in the local belief systems in South-East Asia is the nature of the Indian Ocean maritime network and the influences transmitted through it. It has been argued elsewhere[19] that by the middle of the first millennium AD several crafts which owed their inspiration to the Indian subcontinent were widely practised in South-East Asia. These included brick-making, working in stone, especially the production of images, writing and more secular occupations such as bead-making. It should be remembered that the traditional architecture was in wood. The construction of brick monuments at a variety of sites and the local engraving of inscriptions are further indicators of the extent of Indian influence in South-East Asia. This could not have been the outcome of inviting a few Brahmanas to the royal courts, as has been argued by scholars. It could only have been the result of sustained contacts with a diverse group of traders, missionaries and other occupational groups who travelled with the expansion of the maritime network. Perhaps a reference to the Chinese sources may not be out of place here. According to Chinese historical texts, the plains of Bac Bo were absorbed into the expanding Han empire in 111 BC and around 3 BC parts of central Vietnam were incorporated into the Rinan military commandery.[20] This incorporation into the Chinese empire seems to have influenced Vietnamese socio-cultural development in two ways: one, by 'fostering a receptivity to Chinese cultural leadership among ruling class Vietnamese; and secondly by generating, an instinctive resistance to Chinese and, by extension, to all foreign political interference.[21] This interaction between the Vietnamese ruling elite and the Chinese culture is crucial for an appreciation of the role played by Buddhism in early Vietnamese society.

The introduction of Buddhism is traditionally associated with the founding of four temples and it flourished in Vietnam in the 1st-2nd centuries AD. Chinese records refer to the Hu people–a name applied to foreigners including those from India and Central Asia. It appears that Buddhism spread among the people, at least in part, as a new method of controlling the vagaries of nature in the interests of agriculture. Though it had to compete for political patronage with Confucianism, there is evidence that the Buddhist notion of kingship appealed to at least some members of the ruling elite.[22]

Chinese records also mention the existence in this region from the first half of the 3rd century AD to early in the 7th century AD of a polity which they refer to as Funan. This polity has often been described as a centralised empire by early historians which had its beginnings in a river-settlement governed by a mythical Nāga princess married by the Indian Brahmana Kauṇḍinya. Recent research, especially by Claude Jacques[23] has shown that none of these statements can be accepted as an established fact. Funan was perhaps no more than one of the several chiefdoms in the region dependent on the personal prowess of the chief for its fragile existence.[24] This kind of unity quickly dissolved when an overlord died or lost the confidence of his allies.

The Vo-canh inscription from south-central Vietnam dated on palaeographic grounds between the 3rd and 5th centuries AD has often been associated with the Funanese ruler Fan Shih-man, thus marking a shift towards Brahmanical cults and rituals. The badly mutilated introductory verses proclaim the 'first victories' or *prathama vijaya* of Rājā Śri Māra and his rule over the *prajā* through the traditional means of *sāma-dāna* or conciliation and gifts. Kulke has argued, that this inscription in an illiterate society must have enhanced Śri Māra's status even further...[and] may well have complemented the traditional means of magical authority of a powerful chieftain.[25] Though one could disagree with Kulke regarding the presence of several Brahmanas in the region for legitimizing Śri Māra's claim to power, the inscription nevertheless marks a shift towards Brahmanical ritual.

The shift needs to be studied with relation to the ongoing maritime links between South-East Asia from around the 4th-3rd centuries BC onwards and the diverse nature of influences transmitted through these over time. While Buddhism was the dominant religion both of the ruling elite, as also of trading groups till the 3rd-4th centuries AD, the equation between Buddhism and Brahmanism underwent a change with the emergence of the Brahmanical temple in India under the Guptas in the north and the Iksvakus in the Deccan. This change was not merely a matter of religious ideology, but it had implications for the social and economic fabric as well. The Buddhist monasteries could no longer attract generous donations and political patronage on the same scale as before and the Brahmanical sects were certainly on the ascendancy. Similarly, the identity of trade networks also underwent a change.

The first temples were built of a combination of brick, wood, thatch and bamboo. A temple of this type dedicated to Vasudeva-Viṣṇu appears to have existed in the 2nd century BC at the site of Besnagar, while another contemporary shrine was in evidence at Nagari. Between AD 300 and 600 brick temples were built all over India, but it was under the Guptas in the 4th-5th centuries AD that the temple emerged as the focus of social and economic activity and the first land-grants were made to them.[26] The period was also characterised by the consolidation and expansion of agrarian settlements, thus triggering off a series of inter-related reactions which influenced both the nature of trade in the Bay of Bengal as well as the cultural baggage being transmitted to South-East Asia.

A second issue that is relevant here is that the trading network operating within South-East Asia should be envisaged as an open system involving close interaction with local and regional systems. The emphasis in this paper has been on 'prestige' and imported item as indicated by the available archaeological data. Information on the transportation and exchange of metals, subsistence commodities and agricultural products is not readily available and requires more research.

Similarly, these exchange and trade networks need to be studied with reference to water-craft used in the Indian Ocean in antiquity. It has been argued that a distinct boat-building tradition evolved in South-East Asian waters.[27] Archaeological evidence for this has been recovered, unlike South Asia where maritime archaeology continues to be a neglected area of research.

The result of this interaction would, however, vary with the micro-environment and the level of social stratification of the indigenous society participating in the exchange. It is thus within these parameters that changes in early South-East Asia should be looked at afresh.

## NOTES AND REFERENCES

1. George Coedès, *The Making of South-East Asia*, University of California press, 1969, p. 13.
2. J.G. deCasparis, *India and Maritime South-East Asia: A Lasting Relationship*, 3rd Sri Lanka Endowment Fund Lecture, 1983, p. 7.
3. *Ibid.*, p. 18.
4. H. Kulke, "Indian Colonies: Indianization or Cultural Convergence", H.S. Nordholt (ed.), *Onderzoek in Zuidoost Azie*, Leiden, 1990, p. 21.
5. G. Sontheimer, *Pastoral Deities in Western India*, Oxford University Press, 1993.
6. D. Desai, "Social Dimensions of Art in Early India", Presidential Address, Indian History Congress, Gorakhpur, 1989-90; H. Kulke, *Kings and Cults: State Formation and Legitimation in India and South-East Asia*, New Delhi, 1993.
7. D. Bayard, "The Roots of Indochinese Civilisation: Recent Developments in the Prehistory of South-East Asia", *Pacific Affairs*, 53/1, 1980, p. 98.
8. P. Bellwood, *Man's Conquest of the Pacific*, New York, 1979, p. 183.
9. P. Sorensen, "Kettledrums of Heger Type I: Some Observations", I.C. Glover (ed.), *South-East Asian Archaeology 1986*, University of Hull, 1990, p. 196.

10. A.J. Bernet Kempers, "The Kettledrums of Southeast Asia: A Bronze Age World and its Aftermath", *MQRSEA,* 10, Rotterdam, 1988, p. 153.
11. P. Bellwood, *Prehistory of the Indo-Malaysian Archipelago,* Academic Press, 1985, p. 277.
12. H.P. Ray, *The Winds of Change: Buddhism and the Maritime Links of Early South Asia,* Oxford University Press, 1995, chapt. III.
13. C. Higham, *The Archaeology of Mainland South-East Asia,* Cambridge University Press, 1989, p. 252.
14. L. Malleret, *L'Archaeologie du Delta du Mekong,* Paris, 1962, plates XXXIX-LVI.
15. Ha Van Tan, Oc Eo: Endogenous and Exogenous Elements, *Vietnam Social Sciences,* 1-2, 1986, p. 98.
16. B.N. Mukherjee, "Kharoshti and Kharoshti-Brahmi Inscriptions in West Bengal (India)", *Indian Museum Bulletin,* XXV, 1990, p. 72.
17. Claude Jacques, "Funan', 'Zhenla': The Reality Concealed by these Chinese Views of Indo-China", R.B. Smith and W. Watson (eds.), *Early South-East Asia,* Oxford University Press, 1979, p. 259.
18. I.C. Glover, and M. Yamagata, "The Origins of Cham Civilization", *Archaeology in South-east Asia,* 1995, pp. 167-68.
19. H.P. Ray, *op. cit.,* 1995, chapt. V.
20. I.C. Glover, and M. Yamagata, *op. cit.,* 1995, p. 167.
21. K. Taylor, *The Birth of Vietnam,* University of California Press, 1983, p. xviii.
22. *Ibid.,* pp. 82-83.
23. Claude Jacques, *op. cit.,* pp. 371-79.
24. H. Kulke, *op. cit.,* 1990, p. 17.
25. *Ibid.,* p. 18.
26. V. Dehejia, "Brick Temples: Origins and Development", A.G. Poster (ed.), *From Indian Earth,* Brooklyn Museum, 1986, p. 45; R.S. Sharma, *Indian Feudalism,* New Delhi, 1980, chapt. I.
27. P.Y. Manguin, "South-East Asian Shipping in the Indian Ocean in the First Millennium AD," H.P. Ray and J.F. Salles (eds.), *Tradition and Archaeology: Early Maritime Contacts in the Indian Ocean,* New Delhi, 1996.

# 2

# Prehistoric Art to Folk Art: A Possible Continuity in South-East Asia

D.K. Bhattacharya

Since no human society can be entirely understood without going into its ethno-history, I propose that before we get into the main topic of the present discussion we try to decide the theoretical frame within which the art and culture of Laos can be understood. It is important to realise at this juncture that Laos being a land-locked country surrounded by countries where intensive cultural activities are known from a very early date, will have to depend on explanation of its culture for which one might have to use models of diffusion, transmission and acceptance.

If one can hurriedly scan the work of the diffusionists in the West, one finds generally a hint being given about the fact that a more or less common basis characterises all hunter-gatherer economies *albeit* in comparable ecologies. This approach was later further elaborated by Gordon Childe and this eventually gave rise to what was then termed as *historical materialism.* One of the most important point put forward by almost every diffusionist is that the cultural aspects of a community as indicated by ethnology and archaeology agree to a reasonable degree with the results of linguistic and somatological findings. Experts, however, felt that the distribution of material culture need not show such similarities because of possible differences in material resources available to each community.

It is needless to emphasise the importance of chronology in such attempts. That is, not only can the direction of cultural transmission be reversed if the chronology is not properly ascertained, but also one can make a mistake in declaring any cultural element as having developed parallelly. The latter approach, which comes in the ambit of evolution, can always be borrowed to explain everything everywhere. Consequently, most of the diffusionists do not approve of evolution to explain culture. For drawing prehistoric evidences we might have to depend on such broad ascriptions of time as, e.g., Lower Pleistocene, which might mean anywhere between 900,000 and 400,000 years, or Middle Pleistocene, which is between 400,000 and 150,000 years or the like. But for working on ethnographic transmissions we do not have even these broad estimations of time. Written historical or epigraphic sources come handy for estimating a possible date but this can be used only when one is dealing with early historic or medieval societies. Unlike these possibilities working with pre-literate societies become extremely difficult because here beyond showing broad similarities between cultures, one cannot comment on any of the other issues on which a diffusionist has to also comment. A diffusionist has to also consider the reasons and direction of diffusion as much as the way it is effected. That is, whether political pressure was brought upon an ethnic group to change consequent to invasion, or whether change occurred due to ideas travelling through traders or even through racial mixture are some of the ways in which diffusion can be effected. The process of integration of the exogenous cultural element within a community can take entirely different shades depending on the different ways in which it is effected. Working with the pre-literate societies, one has to compromise with many of these sectors, primarily because one can barely work out the culture of a community during 'pre-contact' days. Even for that matter, if there had, at all, been any contact or not may be disputed.

One of the significant contributions on the diffusion of culture traits is that of Heine Geldern's 1954 study entitled, *Die Asiatische Herkunft der Südamerikanishen Metalltechnik.* He was able to support his arguments with a wealth of archaeological parallels from both sides of the Pacific Ocean. He could demonstrate that contacts between the coastal areas of China and Peru began towards the end of the 8th century BC. Further, this was also possibly the time that working with gold entered South America. Geldern had laboriously compiled various cultural traits and their range of variations between Costa Rica to northern Argentina and demonstrated a fairly intensive connection between these areas over a long period of time. No parallels can really be explained without actually demonstrating historical connections. Yet when one observes such similarities between tribes which may be physically very far away from each other, one can certainly hypothise the possibility of diffusion. Heine Geldern, elsewhere, had also commented on the possibility of a connection of Bihar, Bengal and the states of North-East India with South-East Asia on the ground of the occurrence of shouldered celts in both the regions during Neolithic and later periods. In the matters of human cognition and ideology, as well, such parallels are not difficult to come by but most of the diffusionistic studies barely considered these phenomena. In the present discussion, therefore, an attempt is being made to consider all prehistoric evidences to seek an explanation to it.

The ability to depict through visual pattern is specific to man as a species. What he depicts and how he depicts are issues which have so far not been adequately understood. Although Kapila Vatsyayan and some other selected few have made brave attempts to explain such depictive practices in both Indian performing as also in visual folk art; yet such attempts when extended to prehistoric visual art can create a gross logical fallacy—because it will essentially entail imposing our cognitive perception into the products of an alien cognitive world or culture. In the field of prehistory as well, researchers usually avoid working on rock-art primarily because our tools of classification and analysis are not suited to handle art data. D.D. Kosambi (1962) for the first time made an attempt to examine various depictions from the Syro-Hittite seals comparing them with available texts and inscriptions in order to establish the primeval mother-goddess principle spread over a large cross-cultural stretch. Subsequently, Yashodhar Mathpal (1975) initiated a laborious study of Bhimbetka cave paintings. His main attempt was to create a meticulous documentation and then venture on a socio-enonomic reconstruction of life ways in the period of depiction. V.S. Wakankar (1957) of Ujjain, who first brought to light these rock-art evidences, primarily continued this effort and discovered several newer frescos from Morena, Bhind, Devas and other southern and western Madhya Pradesh regions. After Wakankar's demise, the Ujjain school has been involved in basically classifying forms and functions of art in order to develop chronology for these evidences.

Rock-art usually has a romantic appeal and its analysis had no binding of a tested methodology for interpretation. The combination of these two factors has led to diverse and apparently convincing interpretations, which could not always stand to close scrutiny. Two things emerge from these rock-art studies done so far in India. One since microliths have been found around these shelters, it was invariably assumed that these art evidences are the workmanship of a community which lived during early Holocene period. No archaeologist was ever willing to entertain a possibility of microlith using hunter-gatherers surviving in these rocky forests till probably as late as the arrival of iron. The existence of hunting tribes like the Baigas in the immediate neighbourhood was not an archaeologist's problem and hence was entirely left to the anthropologists to explain. Unfortunately anthropologists in India at that time were so preoccupied with social theories that ethno-history was basically a non-issue to most of them. As a consequence, interpretation of rock-art in India followed a typically Anglo-French method of analysis.

We had always been too eager to look to the West Asian civilisations for explaining the origin and spread of our indigenous culture. Right from the time of Marshall and Mackey, both the origin and decline of Indus Valley culture were traditionally explained with forces from the West. This sets in a kind of limitation to our thinking if extended beyond a limit. Yet we seem to be till now broadly guided by this set rubric laid down during our colonial past. During 1950s and 1960s this pattern became such an obsessive angle that once an archaeologist friend of mine commented—"It seems we had nothing which was our own. For everything had to come to us from the West." That India had developed distinct and diverse eco-adaptations in some specific zones and contributed heavily in metamorphosing West Asian influences are now beginning to be considered by a handful of archaeologists. Further, such an approach made us totally ignore the possibility of other existing corridors of culture flow. That India also acted as a springboard for population migration and/or contact with South-East Asia consequently never got adequately investigated.

Countries in the entire erstwhile Indo-China, in this regard, act as excellent laboratories where these cross-cultural contacts could be fruitfully studied. However, this needs an extremely careful approach primarily because pre-Vedic Hinduism in India was deeply embedded in tribal belief structure. And such belief structures are as varied as the number of ethnic communities practising them. Most western analysts are likely to miss this point when considering contacts with India.

That Laos had been receiving cultural influences from both India and South China cannot be contested, but the nature of such influences would be difficult to elucidate unless we try to isolate the pre-Vedic tribal influences from those of the classic or Vedic and Puranic influences and finally those that arrived with the beginning of the Buddhist period. If Buddhism arrived in Laos from South China and Thailand then the first Indian contacts must have preceded them. Thus, an attempt to understand Indian influence in the rock-art of Laos necessarily involves a better understanding of the Mesolithic hunter-gatherers present in the eastern longitudes of India.

With this background in mind we will like to look at the Chota Nagpur region in India. This is an area of densely forested hills in south Bihar and extends into Orissa and West Bengal. No large rivers pass through this region, yet in the north the mighty Gaṅgā, in east the Ajay and in the south the Burhabalang encompass the area. Prehistory of this region has been reported in numerous publications from the time of Valentine Ball (1870) to Sarat Chandra Roy (1915) and later by Dilip K. Chakrabarti (1993). Palaeoliths, Mesoliths and Neoliths have been recorded from numerous sites earlier by these authors. The present author, on re-examination, felt that at least some of these evidences are extremely late in occurrence and are vastly overlapping in these regions. That is, if Palaeoliths occur between about 200,000 and 8000 BC; Mesoliths between 8000 and 4000 BC and Neoliths between 4000 and 2000 BC for India as a whole, in Chota Nagpur all these stages are squeezed within a duration of probably 60,000 to 1000 BC. Further, the Mesolithic period seems to continue even after copper and iron have been developed elsewhere in the valleys. Since Chota Nagpur is rich in metal ores, it is not difficult to assume that the ore prospecting communities which might have grown into chiefdoms around 1500 BC started using these late surviving Mesolithic hunter-gatherers as cheap labour. Even today the tribals are being used in the same manner by tendu leaf, limestone or wood contractors. These spasmodic and short period contacts do not substantially change tribal cultures but products of "higher cultures" (such as metal utensils, torch, transistors or the like) do get transferred. The inordinately long period of Mesolithic culture in Chota Nagpur, therefore, can be taken to demonstrate a pure hunting-gathering economy entering in symbiotic relationship and hence skipping classical stages of Neolithic and Metal ages. Archaeological evidences also indicate such a possibility when microlithic tools are found in association with heaps of copper and iron slags.

This extended period of survival of a Mesolithic hunter-gatherer economy resulted into numerous waves of migration all over South-East Asia. Root crop adaptation and fishing provided a kind of security of supply which could maintain small dispersed bands and these are not very congenial to the development of compact village society. At best fragmented lineages must have maintained their usual social interactions. The ecology available beyond 80° E in the west could not provide this kind of subsistence to which they had perfected their technology as also the social mores. Consequently, migration was possible only to the south or the east.

Laos and Cambodia provided areas of comparably less population density and enormous bio-diversity. Archaeological evidences of Mesolithic tools from this region have so far not been studied with the specific aim to see their comparability with east Indian evidences. But one could see that *Hoabinhian* is a very late surviving microflake and microblade culture of Indo-China which bears strong similarity with cultural evidences known from Garo hills and Manipur Valley. In fact, if myths can be taken to reconstruct the social history of any micro-region, one of the myths of the region provides some excellent hints of the manner of population movement in Laos. The myth describes how two brothers set out in the lookout of suitable site for settlement (the myth does not describe where these brothers came from). They chose the area between the rivers Mekong and the Nam Khan. The elder brother marked the area first but the younger brother drove him out and occupied the area for himself. The elder brother and his followers went off into the surrounding hills and started living there in scattered settlements. It is historically claimed that these hill dwellers are the ancestors of the minority ethnic groups which constitute nearly 30-40 per cent of the population of Laos today. The fertile valleys are occupied by the Thai speaking later migrants. The relationship of the Laos towards these minorities contains elements of tolerance, fear of their expertise in the supernatural and economic exploitation of natural flora and fauna. They admit that they are able to live in peace only because the hillfolks keep the malevolent powers of the region at bay. Even today, the term of reference used for a menial labour is the same as that used for an elder brother in keeping with the myth.

With such a possibility of ethnic movement, one would like to examine if rock-art—both motifs and symbols, could sustain the contact theory. Here I must hasten to add that human settlements of a much earlier date are known from Lampang Valley in north-east Thailand which is not exactly very far off from Laos. What we are trying to demonstrate is the possible population contact that must have taken place in repeated waves from around 5000 BC to 1000 BC. This is also the period when simple hunter-gatherers were being constantly pushed into inhospitable terrains by later settlers.

A theory of possible contact requires solid evidences which are neither very easy to come by nor are always absolutely confirmative. My contention, here, is to consider rock-art as the proof of such contacts through time. But for this, one needs to demonstrate that visual depiction is a continuing tradition and merges with folk art in the younger phase of history. The recent discovery of rock-art from the tribal heartland of Chota Nagpur (districts Nawada and Giridih in Bhiar, India) by Col. A.K. Prasad throws open such a possibility which needs a thorough and systematic study. Rock-art of Chota Nagpur is specially significant because here we have a living tradition of rock painting practised by the tribals during marriage which they call *Kohbar*. Secondly, Col. Prasad has also discovered an engraved sentence in Kharosthi script in one of the painted rock surfaces. This script has been subsequently confirmed by B.N. Mukherjee—an eminent expert in epigraphy. These two special features almost prove beyond doubt that the rock surfaces which provided the canvas for expression of human mind did not suddenly become non-functional. They continued to be used in different ways, for different purposes and finally merged with the contemporary folk traditions. Such a view has so far never been entertained in Indian prehistory probably because of the lack of adequate research tools to deal with such vastly different cultural worlds. During 1980-90, Lewis-Williams for the first time attempted to work out a continuum theory in Khoisan tribes of south-west Africa. According to these studies tribal rock-art is essentially and entirely shamanistic and reflects the trance experiences. Naturally, these tend to be highly stylised and distorted. Such abnormal experiences impose a greater strength by the very fact of being enigmatic. It was easy to bring together diverse and dispersed tribal groups with these symbols which were not identifiable with any specific tribal group and yet showed vague similarity with every tribal area of cognition. Symbols, as Victor Turner (1967) will like to see, are the "landmarks...that connect the known with the unknown" and are used in life crisis rituals. Tribal art, whether in Africa, Laos or India, under this logic will have to be considered as human efforts which evolve through a complex tapestry of regulatory symbols that serve the purpose of controlling deviations within a culture. Since these deal with basic anxieties, as African tribal art shows, these also serve the purpose of removing conflict between bands of competing groups. After all, what better way can there be to appease your enemy than demonstrating that you believe in the same spirits as he does, no matter even if the spirits have different myths in the two groups. We have numerous such examples in the ethnographic records from India. Günther Sontheimer (1976) has described the Khandoba deity of western Maharashtra who has two wives—one from a hunter-gatherer tribe and the other from an agro-pastoral caste. Thus, Khandoba acts as a divine *icon* to replace *competition* by *co-operation* between two distinct forms of economies. One does not require swords or sharpen political institutions (unlike Bronze Age Sumeria or early dynastic Egypt) to form a mosaic of tribal groups. Whether it is the *Gawan Deoti* of the Oraons of Chota Nagpur or the *Phi* of the Laos hill tribes, they all are more malevolent than benevolent and they all require to be appeased by animal sacrifice and they also merge with the dead ancestors.

Bulu Imam (1995) first described an elaborate custom of rock-art practised in a village named Isko in district Hazaribagh. Subsequently this was published by INTACH, reproducing all the motifs painted by the tribal as including those which were painted by them in their *Kohbar* custom. Subsequently, I visited the region with a small grant from Indian Council of Historical Research, New Delhi. I collected ethnographic accounts of these tribal paintings and compared them with the prehistoric paintings discovered by Col. Prasad. The re-examination of all these evidences at once makes one point quite clear. And that is as follows:

> Depiction on rock surface with ochre paste is a living and continuing tradition in Chota Nagpur. The motifs chosen are always animal forms including birds and reptiles. Human representation is, by far, rare but curvilinear lines sunrays, or geometric lines are not unknown. According to Khaita Munda, an eighty year old tribal from the same region, the bride before the actual marriage ceremony is required to decorate a bridal chamber where the newly-wedded couple spends their first night together.

This is explained as the process by which evil spirits are cast off from the conjugal life of the newly-wedded. The canvas used to be always rock shelters or caves in good old days. Naturally, the couple would also spend their night alone in such secluded area. This also tested the manly courage of the groom to protect themselves from wild animals. Now the tribals have moved to the valleys, the *Kohbar* is more often than not done in an isolated hut in the periphery of the village. Recently the Munda tribals have started a new technique of art called *Matti Pata* or mud leaf technique. This involves coating a surface with mud and then executing the art with a comb or sharp stick. Incidentally, in one of the rock-paintings reported by Col. Prasad from Kauakol (district Nawada) I found half of the rock surface covered with approximately 2 mm thick mud plastering. There are some animals painted below on the bare rock which is now half covered with mud. Over the plaster, sun motif along with series of broad lines has been painted with the same ochre paste. Reptiles among all the motifs seem to be the most recurrent depiction in the *Kohbar* ritual. Often these reptiles are filled with fish skeleton like chevron marks. There are some cases where the reptiles are shown with feathers or furs and have bird-like tails. Bulu Imam sees a strong resemblance of the reptile motif with Austroasian and South-East Asian dragon motif. It is not unnatural to encounter serpent and iguanas in the dry deciduous as also rain forests. The long co-existence of hunter-gatherers in either kind of ecology is bound to create symbols with ascribed values for these creatures. In fact, the Australian High Commissioner in Delhi, Mark Thomson was so impressed by the similarity of this art with Australian tribal art that he created a special funding for their study.

From Indo-China region, such rock-art evidences need to be explored urgently and stylistic features compared with Chota Nagpur *Kohbar* art. The karst uplands of northern Thailand are still occupied by hunter-gatherers and these also abound in prehistoric cave sites like those in the Banyan valley. Similarly Kanchanaburi province and Khong stream areas show strong possibility of such prehistoric practice being continued as a living tradition. I shall finally end by noting that Khok Phanom Di, which is one of the best excavated sites near the Gulf of Siam shows a late layer containing ceramic evidence between 500 BC and AD 900 (Higham, 1989). The incised motifs used as decoration in many of these pot-sherds compare well with our *Kohbar* decoration technique.

# 3

# Champa: An Outpost of Indian Culture

M.N. Deshpande

From almost the beginning of the Christian era, India has played a unique role in the socio-religious and cultural life of the whole of Asia. She has been responsible for weaving a variegated fabric to clothe the Asian countries with a garment which is distinctive for each region yet bearing an indelible imprint of Indian culture. This process, called 'colonisation' by some, was in essence a spontaneous and peaceful process of sharing her spiritual and material attainments with her near and distant neighbours. Thus, it would be seen that there was, at no stage, a design to overrun South-East Asia with a view to establishing political hegemony or to disturb the established social order of any region. Bernard Groslier,[1] the learned author of 'Indo-China' in the 'Art of World Series', has made a very significant observation about Indian expansion in Indo-China. To quote:

> It was one of the most important civilising movements of ancient times, worthy to compare with the Hellenisation of the Mediterranean world. And India can be justly proud to have spread the light of her understanding over such distant lands, lands which without her might have remained in darkness.

Among the many countries that came under the spell of Indian influence was Champa of that part of the present day, war-torn Vietnam, which is known as Annam. The ancient name of this region as Champa[2] occurs in many Sanskrit inscriptions of that country as *Campādeśa* while the kings are mentioned as *Campeśvara, Campākṣoṇīśvara,* or *Campāpuraparameśvara.*

It can be said without doubt that Champa first felt the impact of Indian culture as early as the 2nd century AD. It is a matter of common knowledge that the prosperous trade with the Far East which began about this time attracted a large number of enterprising Indian merchants and princes to migrate to these regions and establish themselves as pioneers in the field. Before long they identified themselves with these developing countries and soon came to the forefront as political and economic stabilisers of the region. *Periplus*[3] mentions trade-routes from three harbours on the eastern coast near Masulipatam across the Bay of Bengal to the Eastern Peninsula.

## RÉSUMÉ OF PREVIOUS WORK

It was not possible to present a very clear picture of such a continuous cultural contact between India and Champa[4] till the discovery of the numerous Sanskrit inscriptions and other researches in the art and archaeology of that region. The inscriptions were originally published in French in the last decade of the preceding century. This work was further supplemented by Parmentier who carried out large-scale excavations on the sites of the Buddhist monastery at Dong-duong (Indrapura) and the Hindu temple establishments at Mi-son and Po-nagar and published his first volume dealing with Cham monuments (*Inventaire descriptif des monuments Cams de I'Annam*) in 1909. G. Maspero published in 1928 a monograph called *The Kingdom of Champa* (*le Royaume du Champa*) tracing the history of the kingdom from the earliest times till its conquest by Annamites in AD 1471. The art of Champa was further studied by Parmentier and the results of his researches are contained in *Inventair Archaeologique de I'Indo-Chine II, Monuments Chāms de I'Annam* (Texte: tomes I-II, Planches: 2 albums, 1918-19). P. Stern in his book *the Art of Champa and its Evolution* (*L'art du Champa ancient Annam et son evolution,* Toulouse, 1942), reclassified the monuments of Champa and its sculptures and presented a new chronology based on the study of decorative motifs. The latest work on this subject is by J. Boisselier (*La Statuaire du Champa,* Paris, 1963).

## PRINCIPAL CENTRES OF INDIAN INFLUENCE

The ancient Indo-Cham kingdom of Champa whose inhabitants spoke a language of Indonesian group came into existence towards the close of the 2nd century AD near the Vietnamese city of Hue situated almost in the centre of the eastern coastline. The kingdom extended over the entire length of the Indo-Chinese peninsula from the mountainous area known as the Annam-portal in the north to the Mekong Delta in the south. Its centres being: (1) Amarāvatī corresponding to the Vietnamese province of Quang-nam; (2) Vijaya corresponding to Binh-dinh province; (3) Kauthara corresponding to the province of Nha-trang; and (4) Pāṇḍuraṅga corresponding to Phan-rang. These places were successive centres of political authority and it would be interesting to refer to the monumental remains and other antiquities found at these centres and in their vicinity especially with a view to studying very briefly the archaeological wealth of Champa so as to trace their cultural inspiration from India.

The oldest Sanskrit inscription of Champa is attributed to a king who called himself the delight of the family of Śrī-Māra (*Śrimāra...rāja-kula-nandana*). The record which is partly in a developed *kāvya* style and in the ornate Sanskrit metre *vasantatilakā* is attributed to about the 3rd or 4th century AD. Found at Vo-canh, its contents are not very clear, but it appears to be a donation to a Buddhist establishment.

### Amarāvatī (Quang-nam)

Belonging to almost the same period as the inscription mentioned above, is a fine statue of Buddha in bronze found at Dong-duong (ancient Indrapura) and measuring 1.08 metres in height. The remarkable image has unmistakable affinities with Amarāvatī sculpture which has also influenced the plastic art of Ceylon. The symmetrical disposition of the folds of the *uttarīya* bespeak of an art tradition practised at the Buddhist School of Amarāvatī in Andhra Pradesh. The presence of *ūrṇā,* the curly hair and general stance of the image would suggest an Indian origin. In fact, the image is symbolic of the contact between India and Champa in as much as the first centre of political authority was called Amarāvatī after the Buddhist centre of that name in Andhra Pradesh.

In the region of Amarāvatī (Quang-nam) is noticed the rise of the first historical monarch of Champa by the name Bhadravarman (beginning of 5th century AD). In one of his inscriptions (Mi-son no. 2) he is styled as *Dharma-mahārāja-śrī-Bhadravarman.* Another inscription describes him as having dedicated a temple to Śiva under the name Bhadreśvarasvāmī in an area girted by mountains on three sides, a river on the fourth. The site of the temple is identified with Mi-son, but unfortunately nothing of this earliest temple survives to this day as it was burnt more than once. There are inscriptional references to the successive reconstructions of the temple and the extant remains of a temple of a later date indicate that the temple of Bhadreśvara was the national sanctuary of the Chams.

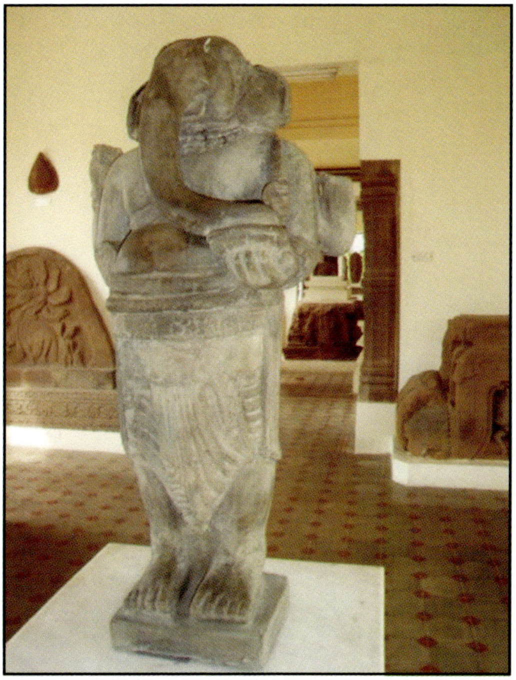

Pl. 3.1. Gaṇeśa, standing position, stone, Mi-son.

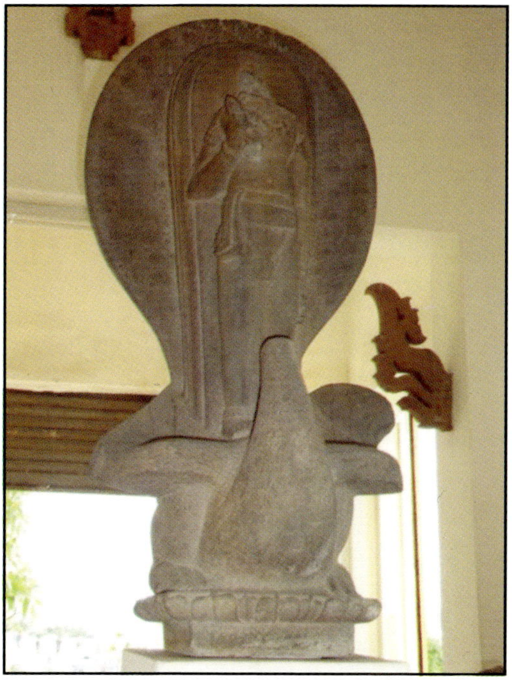

Pl. 3.2. Skanda standing on peacock.

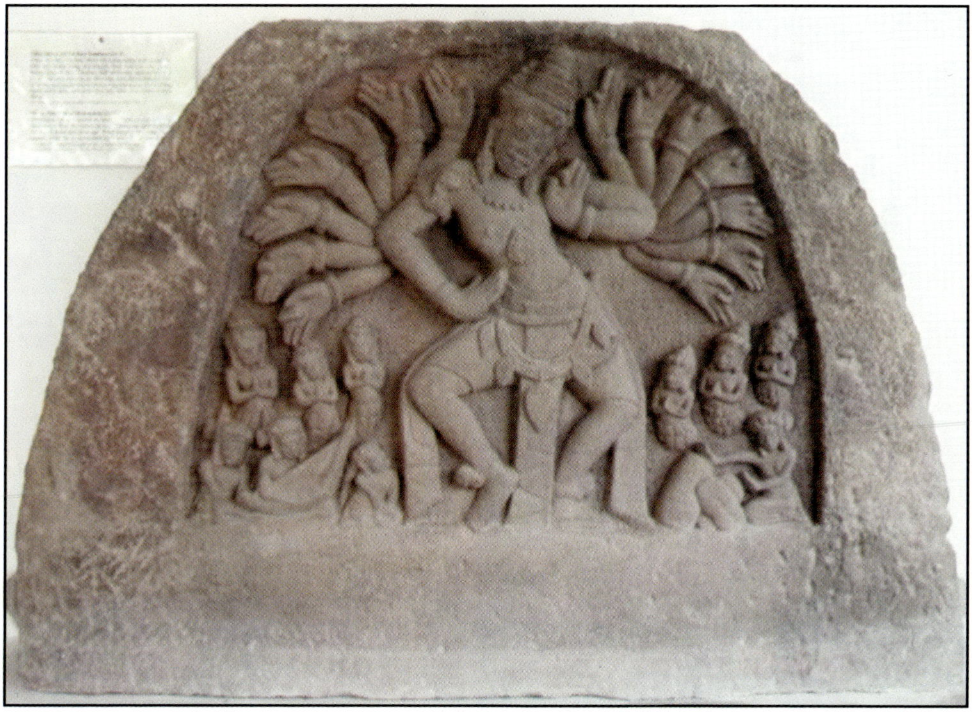

Pl. 3.3. Dancing Śiva with sixteen hands.

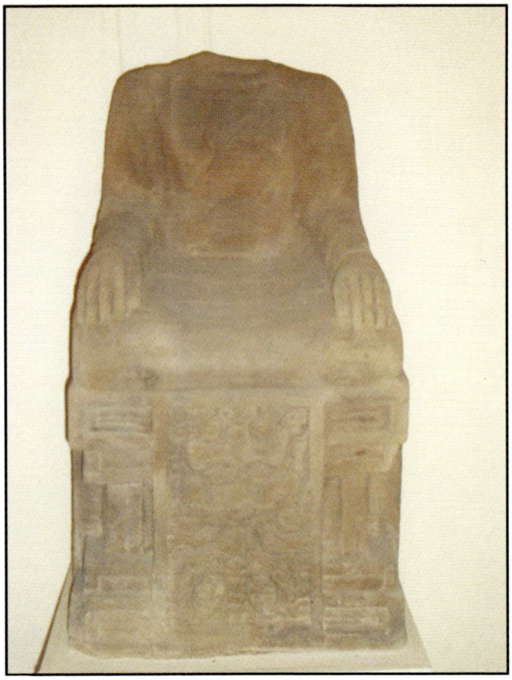

Pl. 3.4. Headless Buddha, Dong-duong.

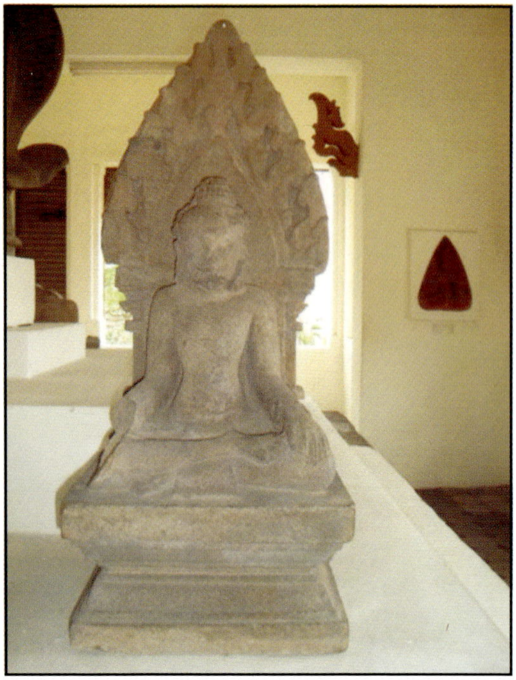

Pl. 3.6. Kubera, Mi-son.

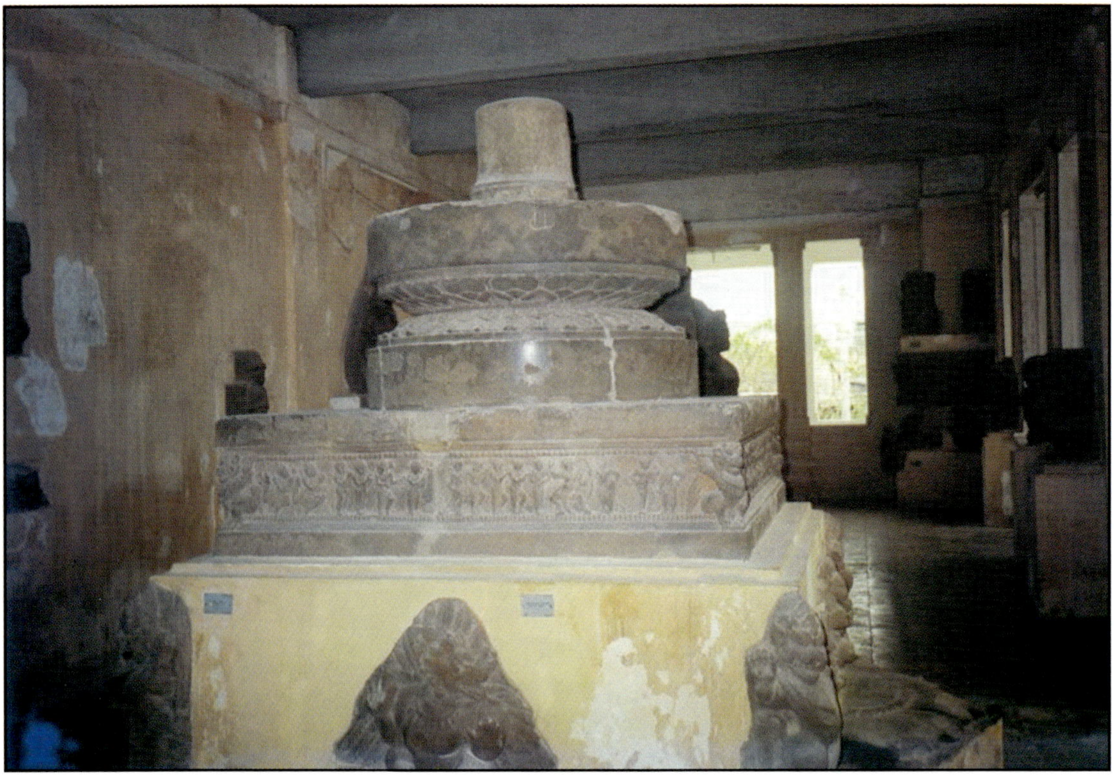

Pl. 3.5. Śiva Liṅga, Tra-kieu.

Early 6th century witnessed the rise of a new dynasty of which the king called Rudravarman (AD 530-72) is said to have belonged to *Brāhmakṣatriya* family. It was during his reign that the famous temple of Bhadreśvarasvāmī was burnt by fire. His successor Śambhūvarman (AD 572-629) is credited to have re-established the temple and renamed it as Śambhū-Bhadreśvara thus adding his own name to that of the original founder.

The first examples of Cham temple art which are preserved in the Museum of Tourane, however, belong to the reign of Prakāśadharma (AD 653- *c.* 686) who, during his long reign embellished Mi-son to a great extent. He is stated to have established a temple called Śrī Prabhāseśvara and also erected a temple dedicated to Kubera, the god of wealth.

The temple site of Mi-son contains ruins of over seventy small and big buildings constructed from time to time by the kings of Champa. The group E-I situated in north-east, on the right bank of a stream is the oldest (7th-8th centuries) and the principal temple was meant to enshrine a large sculptured pedestal to support a *liṅga*.[5] The sculptures undoubtedly betray post-Gupta influence.

In one of the Mi-son sanctuaries near a Śiva Liṅga shrine was discovered a standing image of Gaṇeśa belonging to *circa* 8th century. The four-armed figure of Gaṇeśa (Pl. 3.1) standing erect, is a magnificent example of Cham art. Wearing a decorated *graiveyaka* and a cobra in place of *yajñopavīta,* the image by its heaviness and the manner in which the *dhotī* is tied by means of a broad *kaṭibandha* reminds one of the early traditions of fashioning *yakṣa* images in India. The image is almost 0.94 metre in height and is attributed to Mi-son E-5 group of temples. There is no evidence whether Gaṇeśa was worshipped in Śiva temple as an attendant on Śiva or there was a special cult for his worship as an independent deity. However, a 9th-10th centuries inscription of Harivarman I from Po-nagar mentions that a separate temple was dedicated to Vināyaka when the king replaced the image of *Bhagavatī* in the temple. The image of Gaṇeśa in question is now exhibited in the museum of Tourane.

Belonging almost to the same period is another fine stone image of Skanda (Pl. 3.2) standing on a *mayūra* with the plumage forming an oval-shaped *prabhāvalī.* It is also housed in the Tourane museum.

The popularity of Śiva together with Gaṇeśa and Skanda is worthy of note. While Śiva was worshipped in his phallic form and the kings of Champa vied with each other in earning religious merit by installing and consecrating new *liṅga*-images, there are representations of Śiva in human form. Among such images mention may be made of the Śiva image of *circa* 10th century. The image exemplifies serenity and majesty and is indeed a very fine representation of Śiva. The ornate *mukuṭa* enclosing the *jaṭābhāra,* the *karṇa-kuṇḍalas,* the bejewelled *hāra,* the decorated armlets add to its grandeur. It may be mentioned that Śiva is also presented as performing the *tāṇḍava* dance in the Po-klaung Garai temple where it is installed over the entrance doorway as in some of the Indian temples. Naṭarāja Śiva with sixteen hands (Pl. 3.3) is also represented and the panel from Phong-le preserved in the Tourane Museum reminds one of the Naṭarāja panel in Rāmeśvara cave at Ellora, India. The panel would belong to *circa* 9th century AD. The representation of Rāvaṇānugraha-mūrti-Śiva[6] similar to the magnificent panel in Kailāsa at Ellora is also to be seen at Mi-son.

In the 10th century were erected a number of temples at Mi-son on the left bank of the stream. Of these, monuments belonging to group B-1 are well preserved. The old site of the sanctuary of Bhadreśvara-liṅga is marked by two towers, the principal of which is designated A-1. It dates from the beginning of the 10th century and is the largest at Mi-son. Around the main temple are six small temples (three each to its north and south). The temples usually were built in brick though stone was also used in some cases.

The temples B-5 and D-1 belong to the 10th century AD. The standing figures of deities with folded hands between slender pilasters and framed within vertical floral relief decorations characterise this phase which is in fact a decadent phase of Cham art when the centre of political power was shifted southward to Vijaya (Binh-dinh) in about AD 982.

Belonging, however, to the reign of Amarāvatī (Quang-nam), two other centres merit attention. First is the Buddhist monastery of Dong-duong belonging to the last quarter of 9th century. About this time a new dynasty was reigning over Champa from the capital of Indrapura (modern Dong-duong) situated to the south-east of Mi-son. This dynasty was established by Indravarman II (AD 875-98) who was a devout Buddhist. The Dong-duong stelae inscription of Indravarman starts with salutation to Lakṣmīndra Lokeśvara and mentions that the *vihāra* was founded for the sake of *dharma* and for the residence of the *bhikṣu-saṅgha.* The excavations undertaken at this place brought to light the remains of a Buddhist temple far greater in dimension than the largest Hindu temple in Champa. Many images of Buddha (Pl. 3.4) have been discovered amongst which mention may be made of friezes on the pedestal of a sanctuary illustrating the life of

Siddhārtha starting with the episode of his departure on Kaṇṭhaka horse and subsequent episodes such as cutting his hair-locks and giving away of his clothes and ornaments. The crowding of human figures and exuberance of decoration characterised this period.

The second centre was Tra-kieu situated about 35 km south of Tourane. The city is identified with ancient Siṃhapura and was fortified by brick-walls. Remains of eight Hindu temples have been brought to light, of which the principal one belongs to about 10th century. The brick-terrace exposed in the excavations was decorated with sandstone bas-relief depicting male and female dancers[7] in various attitudes together with lions and elephants. The contorted forms of the female dancers are reminiscent of contemporary depiction on the Coḷa and Cāḷukyan monuments in India and are indeed remarkable examples of the plastic art of Champa.

A pedestal of a Śiva *liṅga* (Pl. 3.5) from this place preserved in the museum of Tourane is decorated with a very fine frieze going all-round the basement with the corners supported by grotesque figures having *kīrtimukha* face. The running panel depicts the story of Kṛṣṇa.

### VIJAYA (BINH-DINH)

A reference has already been made to the shifting of the capital of Cham rulers southwards at Vijaya in the 10th century. King Harivarman II (AD 982-98) consolidated his power but the kingdom was destined to suffer due to external aggression and internal troubles, till ultimately the capital was destroyed in AD 1069 by the Annamite emperor Ly Thanh Ton. It was, however, under Jaya Harivarman I (AD 1147-1166) that Champa regained its independence and the later temples at Mi-son and Po-nagar attest such a revival inspired by the architectural style of Angkor Wat. Subsequent struggle for power between the two Indianised States of Thailand and Vietnam resulted in the weakening of both the powers and Champa could not survive long till in AD 1471, Vijaya, the capital town, was captured and this marked the end of the glory that was Champa.

At Binh-dinh are found the remains of a temple, square on plan within the north-east corner of the enclosure wall of the citadel. The spire of the temple is three-storeyed (*tritala*), corners of which are adorned by miniature shrines like the *kūṭas* in the Dravidian temples. Each storey, as also the central portion of the outer-wall of the sanctuary, has a niche surmounted by exuberantly decorated arch like the *śukanāsikā* of the Dravidian temple. This temple belongs to *circa* 11th century.

At Cha-ban, the old capital of Vijaya, there is a 13th century temple known as the 'Copper tower'.

### KAUTHARA (NHA-TRANG)

The Po-nagar group at Nha-trang consists of about eight buildings of which four are still standing. The inscriptions discovered at Po-nagar mention the construction of a wooden temple enshrining a *mukhaliṅga* by a mythical king Vicitrasāgara. It further mentions that this temple was destroyed and king Satyavarman who built another temple in its place installed a new *mukhaliṅga* together with an image of *Bhagavatī* and Gaṇeśa.[8] It is, however, not possible to identify the temple with the extant ruins.

Among the extant buildings, mention may be made of the principal temple which is fairly well preserved and exemplifies the characteristics of the temples of Champa. The temple has a three-storeyed *śikhara* recalling late Caḷukyan style.

### PĀṆḌURAṄGA (PHAN-RANG)

The last centre from where the Cham kings ruled is Phan-rang (Pāṇḍuraṅga). The founder of this dynasty is mentioned as Pṛthivīndravarman who ruled from AD 758 to 73. Among the line of kings, Harivarman (AD 800-820) is mentioned as *rājādhirāja campāpura-parameśvara.* The standing monuments in the Pāṇḍuraṅga area, however, belong to a later period marking the final stage of Cham art and architecture. The Po-klaung Garai temple assigned to the 13th century in its extant form has in its front an inscription carved on three faces of rock of which a part is in Sanskrit. It mentions the installation of a Śiva Liṅga by a prince. The temple which stands on a hill is very well preserved and has a *tritala vimāna* (three-storeyed spire) with miniature curvilinear *śikharas* placed at the corner of each storey. The temple would belong to the reign of Jayasimhavarman IV, who ruled between AD 1287 and 1307.

## CONCLUSION

The reference to the construction of the earliest temple of Bhadreśvara in the first quarter of the 5th century is indeed a very significant development for the study of Indian temple architecture. The late temples of Champa from 8th to 14th centuries deserve to be studied in greater details so as to bring out the similarity with their Indian counterparts, as also to trace possible influences from other Indianised

States of the Far East. Majumdar has suggested that the temples of Badami, Conjeevaram and Mahabalipuram influenced the temple styles of Champa. A closer study is, however, called for.

While Śaivism was popular in Champa, Vaiṣṇavism and worship of Viṣṇu was also prevalent though not to the same extent as Śaivism. The Duong-mong inscription (no. 11) mentions the construction of temple for god Viṣṇupuruṣottama. (इदं भगवतः पुरुषोत्तमस्य विष्णोरनादि-निधनस्याशेषभुवनगुरोः पूजास्थानं श्रीप्रकाशधर्म्मणा कारितम्।।). Viṣṇu is also mentioned as Nārāyaṇa, Hari, Govinda, Mādhava, Vikrama, Tribhuvanākrānta. He is depicted on a pedestal of Mi-son temple in his *Anantaśāyī* form. He also appears riding a Garuḍa and holding *śaṅkha, cakra, gadā* and *padma* on a relief (Boisselier 1963, Figs. 9, 27 and 93). A king by name Jayarudravarman is mentioned as an incarnation of Viṣṇu and the Batau Tablah inscription of Jaya Harivarman I mentions that the king died at Pāṇḍuraṅga.[9] The representations of scenes from the Rāmāyaṇa are also met with at Tra-kieu (Boisselier Figs. 115-117).

Lakṣmī, the consort of Viṣṇu is also referred to as Padmā and Śrī. The representations of Gajalakṣmī are also met with. At Tra-kieu, she is shown as holding two lotuses (Boisselier, Figs. 62 and 111).

Other gods like Kubera (Pl. 3.6), Brahmā, Vāyu and Sūrya are also depicted.

Mahāyāna form of Buddhism was also prevalent in Champa and representations of Buddha and Avalokiteśvara are frequently met with. However, I-tsing mentions that in Lin-yi or Champa the Buddhists generally belong to the *Āryāsammitinikāya* and there are also a few followers of the *Sarvāstivādanikāya.* This would mean the prevalence of Hīnayāna in Champa. On the evidence of inscriptions and sculptures, one can conclude that Buddhism was specially prevalent in the Dong-duong region.

## NOTES AND REFERENCES

1. B.P. Groslier, *Indo-China,* Baden-Baden, Germany, 1962, p. 47.
2. R.C. Majumdar, *Ancient Indian Colonies in the Far East,* Book III, Greater India Society, Lahore, 1927, pp. 11, 15 and 29.
3. Schoff, *The Periplus of the Erythraean Sea,* p. 46.
4. The pioneering work of R.C. Majumdar focused the attention of Indian scholars to the maritime contact of ancient Indians in the Far East and intimate cultural ties between India and Champa in particular.
5. H. Parmentier, "Les Sculptures Chames au Musée de Tourane", *Ars Asiatica,* Paris, 1922, Pl. IV.

6. Jean Boisselier, *La Statuaire du Champa,* Fig. 15.
7. In passing, a reference may also be made to the only Buddhist painting of Thie-khe about 47 km north-west of Hanoi, representing Buddha attended by Bodhisattavas. There are also male and female figurines dressed in costumes similar to that worn by figures in Central Asia. (*Encyclopaedia of World Art,* XIV, New York, 1967, p. 771.)
8. Majumdar, *op. cit.,* inscription no. 22, pp. 41-44.
9. In this context, one is tempted to connect the name Pāṇḍuraṅga with Pāndharpur, a celebrated Vaiṣṇava centre in Maharashtra, the presiding deity of the town being Pāṇḍuraṅga also called Viṭṭhala.

# 4

# The Art of Cham Temples in Vietnam

J.C. Sharma

The awareness about the temples of Champa is extremely poor and it is a pleasure for me that the Indira Gandhi National Centre for the Arts has taken the initiative to organise this Seminar and include a session on the "Art of the temples of Champa". Unfortunately these temples have not received the attention they deserve during the last four decades. This is probably due to the disturbed conditions in Vietnam. Most of the Cham temples are in an advanced stage of decay. A number of them are already destroyed. It is absolutely essential that a major effort is mounted for their restoration. These temples are the few surviving links which can help to study the history of the kingdom of Champa. It would be pertinent to mention here that the temples of Champa neither have the massive dimensions nor the grandeur of Angkor Wat and Borobudur. They also do not have intricate carvings like Bantey Srei or Prambanan. These brick temples, however, are unique. There are very few brick temples in South-East Asia.

French scholars of l'École Française d'Extrême-Orient, Paris, France have done pioneering work on these temples. The works of H. Parmentier (1909) and P. Stern (1942) have been considered as outstanding.

The territory of the kingdom of Champa extended from Deo Ngang Pass (approximately 120 km north of Hue) to Dong Nai Basin (approximately 125 km north of Saigon). Since the northern part of the kingdom changed hands very frequently, most of the major monuments are located in the area between Danang and Phan-ri.

Before explaining the chronological account of the temples of Champa, I would like to discuss the general features of these temples. It would be relevant to mention here that there is no surviving secular monument in the kingdom of Champa.

## GENERAL FEATURES OF THE TEMPLES

The temples of Champa generally follow one basic design. The concept of Mt. Meru, the abode of Gods, seems to have played a very important role in the choice of location for the construction of the temple. They generally face east. No doubt, there are several exceptions, the most notable being the "A" group in Mi-son. A temple complex usually has a sanctum sanctorum which has a square base and pyramidal roof. In Cham language, it is called *kalan*. The *kalan* symbolises Mt. Meru, the centre of universe and the abode of the deities. In some cases, the temple has supplementary structures like *kosha griha* (place for keeping the valuables belonging to the deity) and a place for making preparations for worship. Sometimes, facing the *kalan* or sanctum sanctorum is a *natamandir* which runs from east to west.

The temples of Champa are not very large and they were essentially made for worship only. The sanctum sanctorum normally has a Śiva Liṅga at the centre (Pl. 4.2). The space around is small and sufficient only for devotees to do *parikramā* (ambulatory) of the *liṅga*. The interior walls of the sanctuary are plain but polished. The roof of the interior of sanctuary is like a conical vault formed by a succession of rings which rise in diminishing proportion right up to the top. At about mid-height of the roof, a stone slab is fixed at each corner with a hole pierced at the end. This could probably be for hanging a canopy over the deity.

The *kalan* usually has only one door facing east, the direction of the sunrise, though in some cases we do have temples facing west. The *liṅga* of the idol is placed on a moulded pedestal with water chute (*droṇī*) for draining water used for bathing the deity. The *kalan* of the sanctuary is connected through a vaulted passage to a doorway of stone. A tympanum placed above the door lintel usually has some elaborate sculpture. The doorway is connected to an antechamber or vestibule through a vaulted passage. There are, however, some temples without an antechamber. Both the sanctuary and the vestible are based on a common podium.

The temple is normally square on plan with entrance door front and three blind doors on other sides. In some cases there are only two blind doors. The doors usually have arches which are decorated in various patterns. The decorative patterns on the arches and the walls are a speciality of the temples of Champa displaying a high standard of craftsmanship.

Bricks are used as main construction material of these temples. Limited use of stone has been made particularly for doorframes. Stone members have been inserted for the dual purposes of strengthening and decorating the exterior of the temple. The Chams had achieved highest standard in the technique of brick baking and in the art of brick laying in which they, undoubtedly, had no equals in South-East Asia. The Chinese texts have praised the people of Champa as "masters of brick laying art." Is it a mere co-incidence that even now, the brick-layers of Quang-nam Danang are considered the best in their field in Vietnam? They have probably inherited this traditional skill.

The best testament to the quality of bricks is the fact that some of the temples have survived for over 1,000 years in the tropical conditions with heavy rainfall lasting for six months in a year. The bricks are evenly baked and it is difficult to find even a single brick which is over or under-baked. The most striking feature of the brick construction is the fact that no binding material is visible between the bricks. The absence of any binding material has been a subject of debate among archaeologists. In recent years, a theory has been advanced that most probably a locally available botanical material called *Dipeterocapus alatus roxb* has been used for joining the bricks. This glue served the dual purpose of binding as well as providing additional strength to the walls. The outer wall has also been given a coating of some oil to give protection from the inclement tropical climate. The temples usually have three storeys each storey reproducing the arcade of the lower one with its carvings and decorative figures. The interior of the temples is completely plain. The summit is usually crowned by a stone member. At the height of the glory of Cham power, the roofs of several temples in Mi-son were laminated with gold. There is clear evidence of this during the rule of Indravarman IV in the 12th century. The decorative motifs on the red brick-walls laminated with gold lend a special beauty to the Cham temples, not found anywhere else in South-East Asia.

The roofs of some of the temples in Mi-son do not follow the pattern as explained above. It is, particularly, because of supplementary structures. Some of the temples have roofs. Some Vietnamese archaeologists believe that the shape of the roof takes after Valabhi or Wagon-vault of the Dongsonian bronze drums. The evolution of the architectural style is revealed through changes in the decorative motifs on the outer walls of the temples. There are no basic changes in the plan and design of the temples over the centuries.

## ARCHITECTURE OF THE TEMPLES

G. Maspero in *Le Royaume de Champa* (1928) and E.M. Durand in "Les Archives des Derniers Rois Cham" (*BEFEO*, 1907, VIII) have opined that the Cham art developed in the following four stages:

1. First stage: 192-982, formative stage
2. Second stage: 982-1471 peak stage
3. Third stage: 1471-1698 recession
4. Fourth stage: 1698-1882 decline

P. Stern in *L'Art du Champa et son evolusion* (1942), arranged Cham art in the following order:

1. Mi-son E1 (ancient style)
2. Hoa-lai
3. Dong-duong
4. Mi-son A1
5. Transitional style
6. Binh-dinh
7. Late style or Po-klaung Gerai style

Tran Ky Phuong and Cao Xuan Pho have suggested minor changes in Stern's classification.

## MI-SON E-1 STYLE

This is named after the E-1 temple in Mi-son complex which unfortunately no longer exists. A study of this style is, therefore, primarily based on the E-1 altar found at Mi-son which is presently displayed in the Cham Museum at Danang. The temple follows a square plan paved with bricks with four carefully covered pillars in four corners. Decorative carvings are simple, slightly squarish and there are no false doors. The entrance corridor is very narrow. E-1 style evolved in early 8th century when Champa was a properous kingdom. Some scholars suggest its date around 6th or 7th century. This style shows the evolution of architecture and sculpture of Champa. It shows powerful Indian influence as well as some influence of Khmer and Mon Dvārāvati art. The E-1 style, therefore, shows harmonization of national character with foreign influence. This style culminated in a technique of temple construction with the use of perishable material like wood which was used in the temples at Mi-son. This style ushered in the distinctive local style.

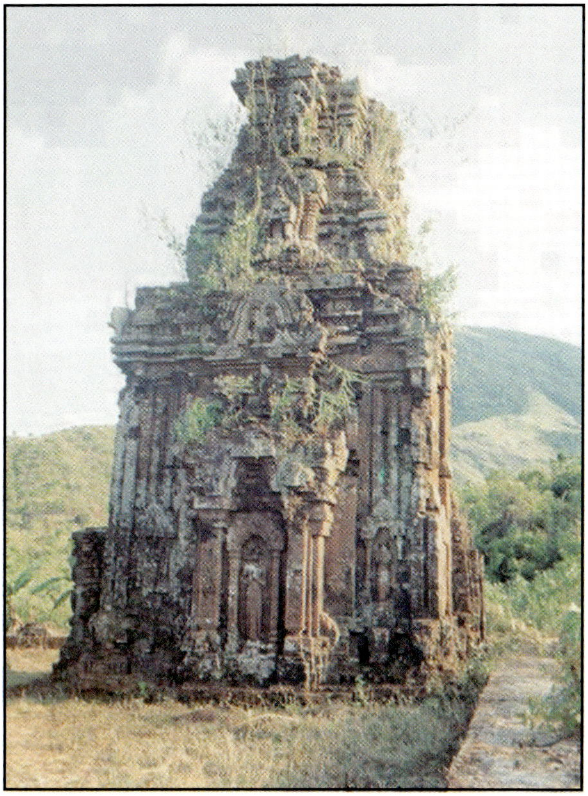

Pl. 4.1. Mi-son B3 type temple.

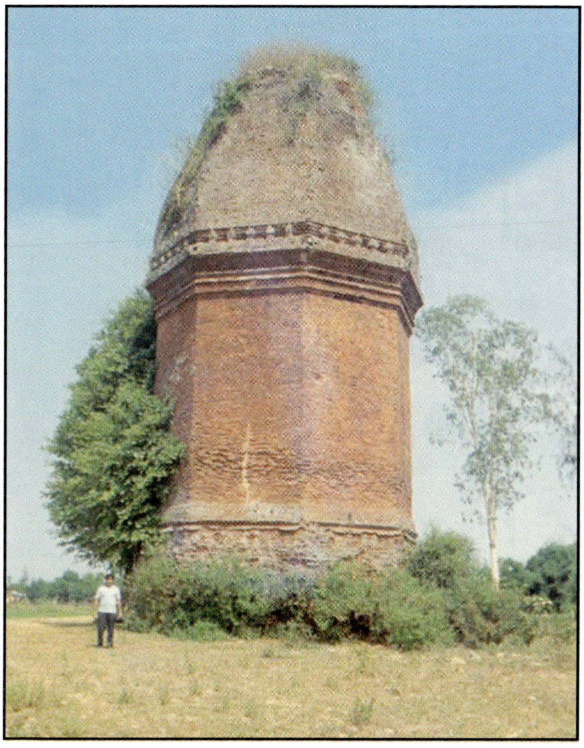

Pl. 4.2. Bang-an temple (western view).

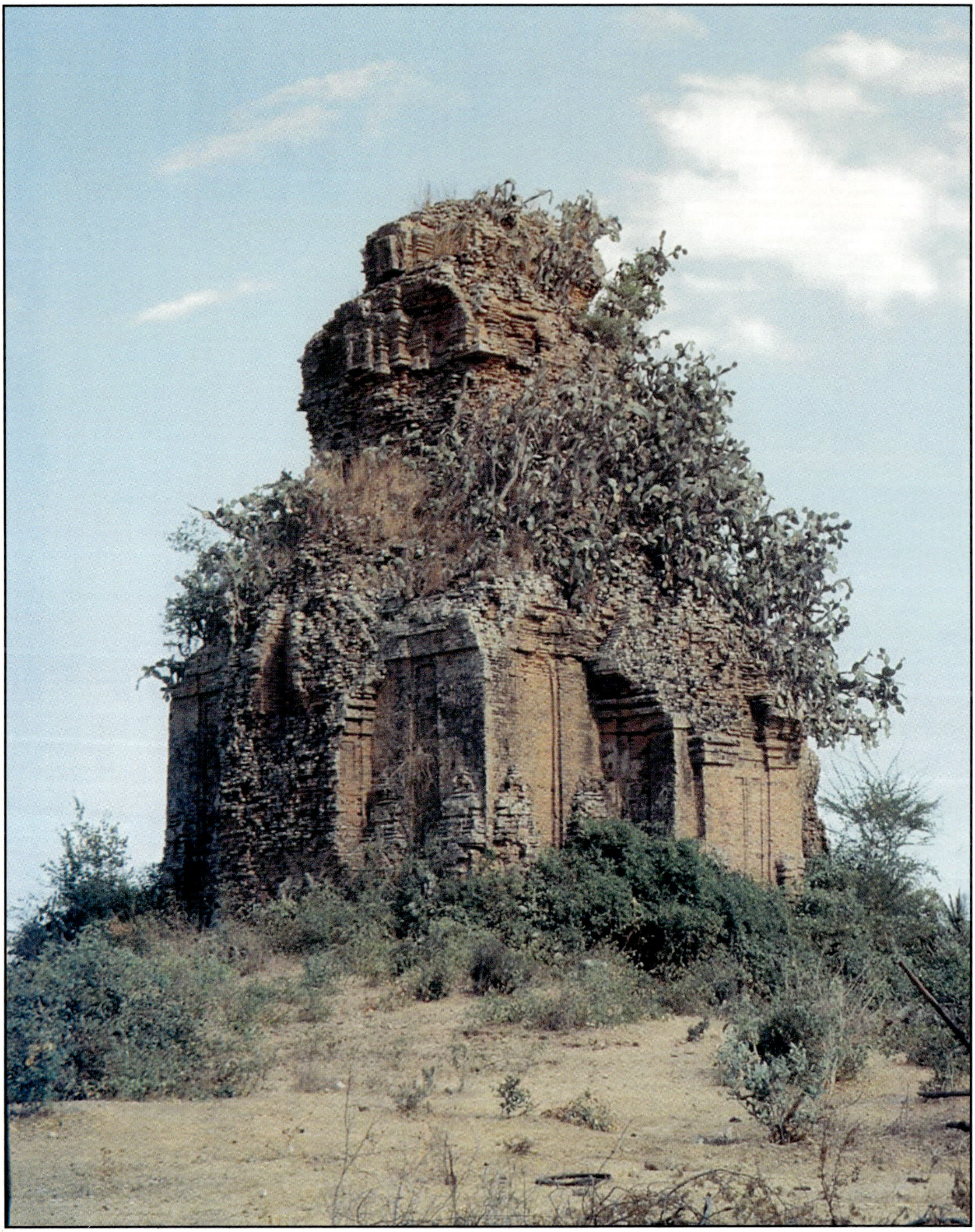

Pl. 4.3. Hoa-lai temple.

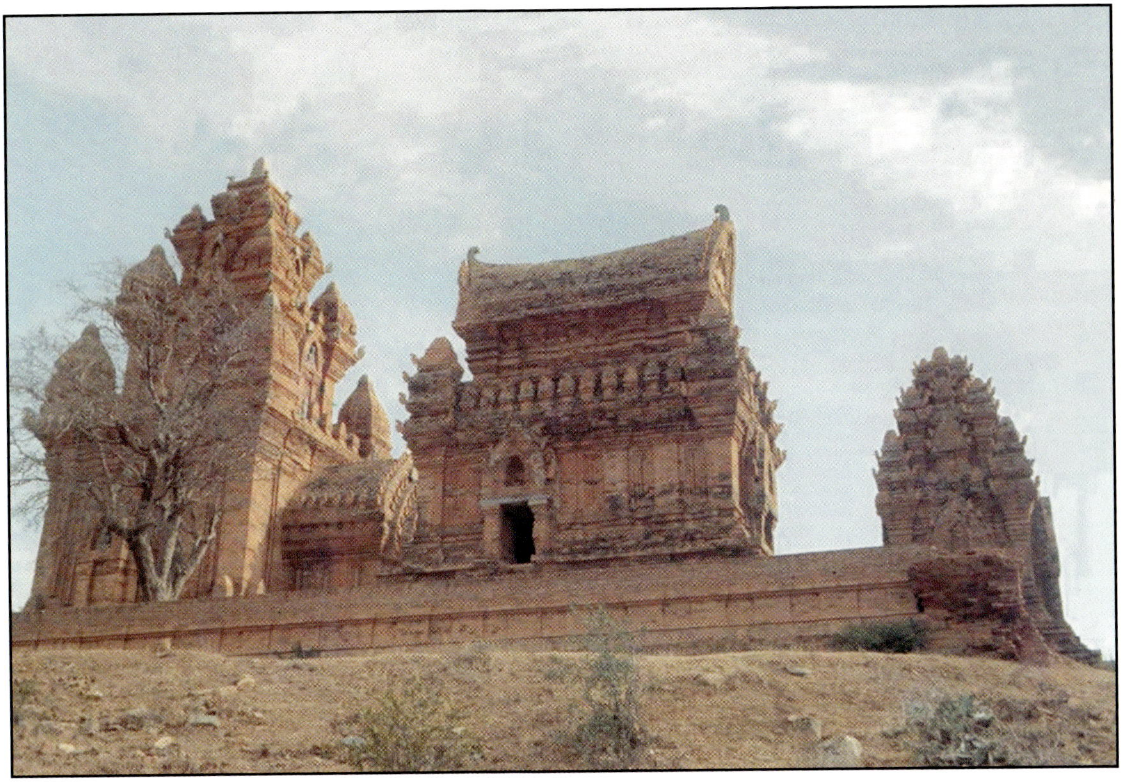

Pl. 4.4. Po-klaung Gerai temple (general view).

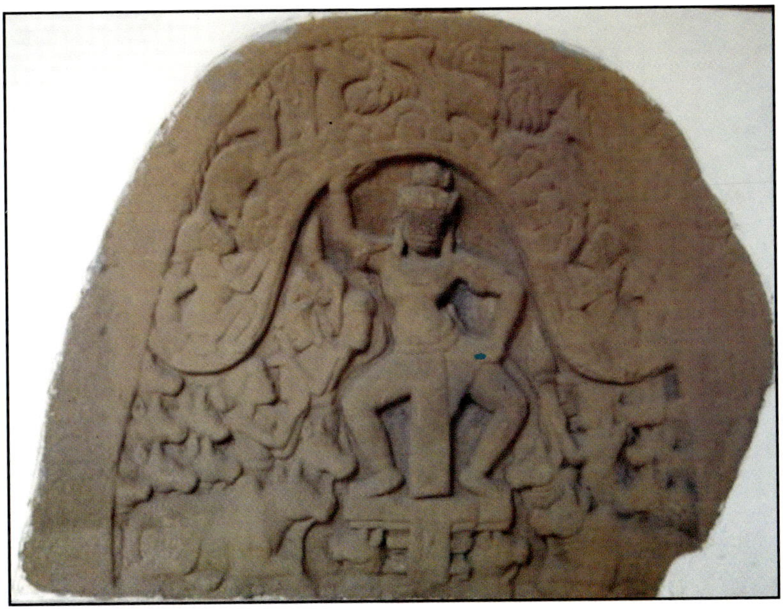

Pl. 4.5. Kṛṣṇa lifting Govardhan mountain, Khuong My, Quang-nam.

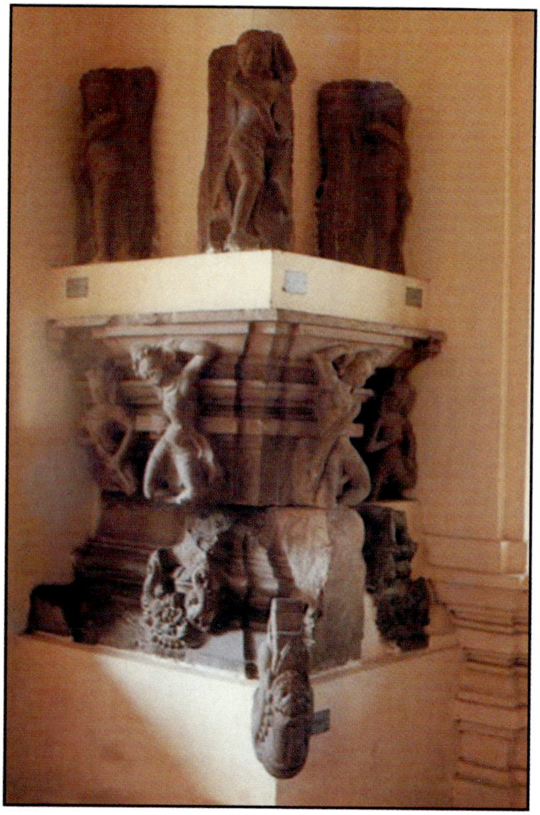

Pl. 4.6. Dancing girl – pedestal, Tra-kieu.

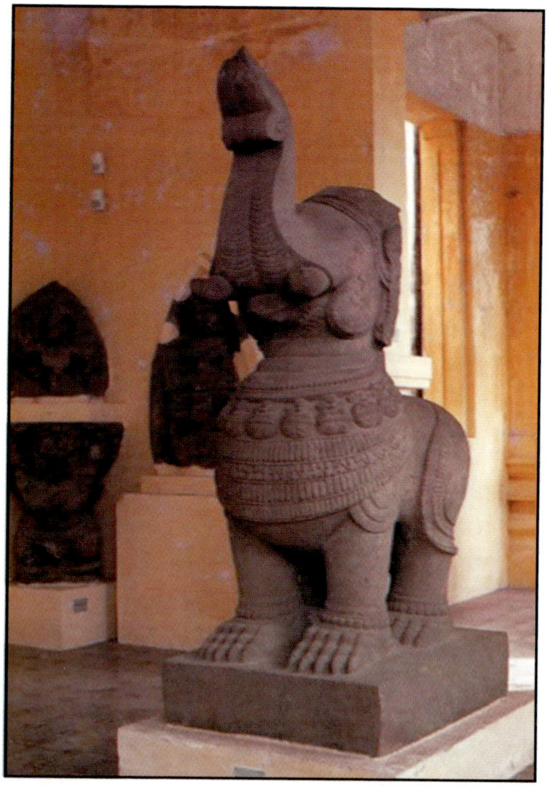

Pl. 4.7. Gajasiṁha, Binh-dinh.

## HOA-LAI STYLE

This style evolved during the late 8th and early 9th century and is named after the temple ensemble at Hoa-lai. The basic plan of the temple remains the same because of the low roof in the shape of a cube (Pl. 4.3). Parmentier has named it as a cubic art. The style shows dilution of the Indian influence and development of native character with some influence of Khmer and possibly Thai. Boisselier is of the view that this style has some Buddhist as well as Javanese influence. I am in agreement with this view, particularly because of the carving of arches which show Javanese influence. Mi-son F-1 and C-7 are among other examples of this style.

## DONG-DUONG STYLE

This style is named after Dong-duong area in Quang-nam Danang province. Powerful influence of Buddhism on Champa during the rule of Indrapura dynasty contributed to the development of this style. Buddhist influence probably led to the construction of a new capital where both religious and secular buildings could be constructed in the same area. Development of this style appears to be the result of conscious efforts to make a break from the past. The native character is strongly represented both in scale and arrangements. This is also reflected in decorative patterns. The altar at the Dong-duong hall in Cham museum depicting various scenes from Buddha's life is a fine example of this style.

## MI-SON A-1 STYLE

Re-emergence of Hinduism as the dominant religion in Champa had its impact on architecture and sculpture. The extremism and emphasis on native character were again replaced by refinment and delicateness. The emphasis is on flowing beauty and harmony, so that the total effect is pleasing to the eyes. During this period, relations between Champa and Java were very close. This is probably the reason for Javanese influence on the works of this period. Temple A-1 is the masterpiece of this style. A lot of attentions have been paid in achieving proper proportions and pillars and pilasters have been lengthened in order to achieve this objective. Sandstone slabs with beautiful carvings of *apsarās*, *garuḍas*, flowers and leaves have been crafted to enhance the beauty of the structures. There is a re-emergence of the traditional beauty of E-1 style along with the Javanese influence. This fusion has created a style of its own. A common motif for this period is the image of Makara Kāla vomiting a deer.

Mi-son B-3 type (Pl. 4.1) is a small beautiful temple dedicated to Skauda, the son of Śiva. B-5 temple in Mi-son complex is also a very fine example of this style. The door of the temple is facing north and windows are on the east and the west. Some archaeologists are of the view that the Valabhi (boat-shaped) roof is possibly the result of the influence of Dongsonian culture because similar motifs are also found on Dongson bronze drums. The *kalan* and *mandapa* of C-1 and the D-1 temples at Mi-son are also good examples of this style.

## BINH-DINH STYLE

The capital of Champa was moved to Vijaya in the 11th century. Hence, most of the monuments of this style are found in the Vijaya area. Champa also had very close contact with Khmers leading to Khmer influence on architecture. Some influence of Dai Viet is also witnessed. This is a period of transition between A-1 style and full development of Binh-dinh style. A number of scholars have called it Po-nagar style. After the famous temple of Po-nagar at Kauthara (Nha-trang) during transition period, we find some influence of A-1 style. However, the monuments of this period do not have the same degree of symmetry and refinement. One interesting feature is the disappearance of cupolas and the false doorways. We also no longer see beautiful pilasters and architraves, which are now suppressed into simple motifs. We no longer find a fine balance between architectural design and sculpture, to achieve an overall effect. The buildings of this period look somewhat heavy and lack delicateness, grace and charm of the A-1 style. Temple ensemble of Po-nagar is a representative example of the transition period. Some of the other examples of this style are Banh It (Silver tower), Canh Tien and Duong Long. The temple ensemble of Po-klong Gerai (Pl. 4.4) constitutes a class by itself. These temples retain some of the delicateness, grace and grandeur of A-1 style and their location makes them look truly majestic. These temples are in a good state of preservation. One of the most important Cham festivals Kate is celebrated here. It would be important to mention that the present name of most of the temples has either been given by the French scholars or the Vietnam population. We do not have definite information about the original name of these temples. After the temple of Po Rome, hardly any temple of significance was constructed in Champa. This is undoubtedly due to the decline in power and prestige of the kingdom of Champa.

## SCULPTURES

The sculptural art of Champa was closely linked with the architectural constructions. The sculptural works are primarily in two categories. The first category includes carvings and decorations on outer walls, cupolas, pillars and pilasters. The second category encompasses *liṅgas*, statues and carvings on columns, tympanums and panels grafted in the exterior of the temple. The sculptural work of the first category is mostly on bricks, and of the second category, on sandstone. There are some sculptural works also in bronze and wood. However, very few examples of bronze or wood are available for the purpose of proper study. At present, very few sculptural works of the first category have survived. Unfortunately, a lot of damages to the sculptural works have also been caused by wars, and many statues have fallen prey to the greedy eyes of the antique hunters. For a study of sculpture we, therefore, have to basically depend on the existing monuments and the collection which is on display in various museums. As in the case of architecture, the sculptural art of Champa has been classified differently by various scholars. For our purpose, we will go by the following classification adopted by Cao Xuan Pho (1988):

1. Mi-son E-1 (first half of 8th century)
2. Hoa-lai (first half of 9th century)
3. Dong-duong (end of 9th century)
4. Tra-kieu (end of 9th to beginning of 10th century)
5. Binh-dinh or Thap Mam
6. Po-klaung Gerai

It is also based on the classification done by Stern.

## MI-SON E-1

This is the first well-defined style of sculpture of Champa named after E-1 temple in Mi-son. It corresponds to E-1 style architecture of 8th to 9th centuries. The finest specimen of this style is E-1 altar which has already been discussed in this paper under architecture. The altar beautifully depicts human and animal figures and the scenes of nature. The dance movements of a dancer are beautifully sculptured at the step of the altar. The altar also shows various aspects of the lives of Brahmin priests. They are shown meditating under tree, praying, playing musical instruments, holding holy books, preaching surrounded by birds and animals, etc. The altar has also beautiful carvings of both big and small animals like tiger jumping up with all its strength, boar trying to stand up, a squirrel on a tree and a monkey listening to a priest.

The birth of Brahmā from the navel of Viṣṇu and standing Gaṇeśa are fine specimens of this art style which are kept in the Cham museum at Danang.

This altar clearly demonstrates the high degree of proficiency of Cham sculptors in carving human figures as well as nature. The influence of Indian art is clearly visible and scholars are of the view that Sanchi and Gupta art style influenced the sculptures of Champa during this period. Some scholars have termed it the early Tra-kieu style based on the sculpture found at Tra-kieu (Siṃhapura) of the 7th-8th centuries.

## HOA-LAI

This style evolved with the building of temples at Hoa-lai and their contemporary buildings at Bich La and Mi-son complex. The important feature of this style is the effort made to give a native appearance to the sculpture. We find on the human figures nose getting a little bit wider, a thick lower lip, moustache and wider mouth. The jewellery and clothes also have a native character. The decorative carvings on pillars and pilasters are other hallmarks of this art style. The carvings on Indian *toraṇa*-type arches over false doors are of high aesthetic standard. There was good harmony between architectural design and sculpture. Excellent overall effect has been achieved by proper placing of carved and plain pilasters along with arches decorated with carved foliage. The sculptures on Mi-son, C-1 and D-1 are other good examples of this style.

The work of sculptors was not only confined to carving on bricks. We have also some very fine specimen of the style on stone. An excellent work of high standard can be seen on a sculpture of Bich La in which Śiva is represented performing *tandava* dance on the tympanum. The sculpture has been able to fully convey the mood of the *tandava* dance by showing Śiva standing in *tribhaṅga* position moving his left arm towards his right.

## DONG-DUONG

As in Dong-duong architectural style, sculptures also show high standard of art. Heaviness and emphasis on native character are clearly evident. The nose is flat with large nostrils; lips are thicker and sometimes have a moustache. The expression in most of the statues is serious and pensive. The carving of foliage also lacks refinement. The attempt is to make a break from the past. The Dong-duong section in Cham museum, particularly the altars depicting scenes from the life of Buddha, are representative example.

## TRA-KIEU

Some scholars have divided the Tra-kieu style in two phases: the early Tra-kieu style (7th to 8th centuries) and late Tra-kieu style (late 10th century). Since the late Tra-kieu style basically depicts revival of the features of the early Tra-kieu style or E-1 style we will mention both as Tra-kieu style. Revival of this style coincided with the revival of Hinduism. Once again there is emphasis on refinement and delicateness. There is re-emergence of foreign influence particularly of the Khmer and Javanese. No doubt, during the early part of the 10th century we find some influence of Dong-duong style. Tra Ky Phuong has classified the sculpture of the early 10th century as Khuong My style after Khuong My temples near Danang. The tympanum of Khuong My temple showing Lord Kṛṣṇa holding Mt. Govardhana (Pl. 4.5) is one of the most beautiful sculptures of this period. Revival of Hinduism also led to carvings of beautiful statues of deities as well as musicians and dancers. Foreign influence is seen clearly on carvings of the pillars and pilasters and *toran* like arches. We once again see an emphasis on refinement. The features are soft and gentle. The carving showing female dancers in *tribhaṅga* (Pl. 4.6) with soft smile on their face is among the finest specimens of the sculptural art of this period. The dancers are shown wearing soft fabric *sarongs* and have *kirīṭa-mukuṭa* as headdress. We once again witness carvings of the statues of animals particularly elephants and lions. The sculptural art of Champa reached its zenith during that period.

## BINH-DINH OR THAP MAM

This style corresponds to architecture of the same style described earlier. The decline in the power and glory of Champa is manifested in the sculptural art of this period. Chanh Lo sculpture of the early 11th century marks the beginning of this style and some scholars opine that it was the transitional period of Tra-kieu to Binh-dinh style. The Javanese influence is no longer seen, however, because of close interaction with Cambodge, some sculptures have Khmer influence. Silver tower (Banh It) has some reliefs, carvings and motifs which exude sense of tranquillity and charm of the preceding style. Duong Long

(Ivory tower) shows the Khmer influence. Some dragon-like motifs show the creeping in of Dai Viet influence.

Considerable attention has been paid to the carving of large statues of animals like Gajasiṁha (Pl. 4.7), Lion, Makara and Garuḍa. Some animals almost appear to be domesticated. Another major characteristic of this style is the carving of the motif of Uroja regarded as their mythical ancestor by Chams. The Uroja carvings are shown vividly but the purpose is not to convey any sensuous impression. We find several works where a row of Urojas surrounds the worship place. The *liṅgas* of this period are usually sculptured together with *yonis*. Some of the *liṅgas* are of massive size. The carving of foliage lacks precision and refinement but bolder approach makes them look lively.

### Po-klaung Gerai

The best examples of this style are the sculptural works at the ensemble of temples at Po-klaung Gerai in Phan-rang area. We notice a further decline in the refinement of carvings. This style is marked by cubical emphasis. The decorative carvings now are meagre and sculpture mainly conveys impression of solidness and unrefined strength. It is the continuation of decline in the sculptural art of Champa.

Some statues found in Gialai Kontum area near the Cambodian border show strong Khmer influence of post-Bayon style. The legs of the statues are fully covered with sampot in Cambodian style.

### Kut

Some scholars are of the view that the Binh-dinh style does not mark the end of the sculptural tradition of Champa. They opine that it has only taken a different direction of development. The sculptural works have taken a completely Cham character and are fully related to common folk. Kut sculpture of Cham cemeteries usually has polished stone without elaborate ornamental carvings. It is possible that there is some influence of Po Dam temples of the 8-9th centuries.

To sum up, it can be said that the temples of Champa represent a unique tradition of art. As mentioned earlier, the temples do not have grandeur of Angkor or the delicatness of Bantey Srei, but they have some unique features. They reveal finest specimens of brick architecture. Carving on brick is not an easy job and the Chams have certainly achieved highest degree of proficiency in the art.

There have been some amount of debate about the Indian influence. Parmentier has underplayed the Indian influence. However, it appears that the basic design of these temples is Indian. The availability of the material for construction, the skill of craftsmen, the local interpretation of religious concepts, and the prevailing political and economic conditions played a very important role in the development of Champan Art.

The earlier temples may have been influenced by some of the brick temples of the Gupta period like the temple of Bhitargaon. Dr. Majumdar has pointed out similarities in the design of roofs of some temples of Mahabalipuram complex and the temples of Champa. Some influence of Amarāvatī style is also well established. To conclude, it would be pertinent to give the following quotation:

> I have undertaken this task to study the Cham culture which these temples symbolise in every respect. The Cham culture was like a beautiful tree that grew out of the seed that was undoubtedly Indian, on the soil prepared by Sa-Huynh culture, nurtured and cared for by Chams with the support of other ethnic groups like Katu, Jerai, Rhade, Raglai, and Churu. The influence of Cambodge, Java and the Dongsonian and Dai Viet cultures provided the fertiliser for the growth of the tree.

# 5

# The Dong-duong Art

Bachchan Kumar

Situated roughly between 18° and 10° N latitudes, Dong-duong lies on the coast of south China Sea. Lying in the central part of Vietnam, it was one of the important provinces in the mighty ancient kingdom called Champa, where Chams introduced a distinct art style during late 9th century AD. In this paper, I propose to highlight the salient features of Dong-duong art style in the wider context of Vietnamese and South-East Asian art.

According to Nilakanta Sastri, the ancient name for Dong-duong was Amarāvatī.[1] Coedés also supports it.[2] The name Amarāvatī indicates that the people of this area had regular contact with the south-eastern coast of India where many schools of Buddhism flourished since the early centuries of the Christian era. The epigraphical record[3] mentions it as a beautiful city of Chams. The ruins of Dong-duong have been found about 22 kilometres south-east of Mi-son in the province of Quang-nam Danang.

A number of papers have been written on Champa, but discussions on the Dong-duong art in the wider context of Vietnamese and South-East Asian art are lacking. H. Parmentier has elaborately mentioned the Chams monuments in his work.[4] Bernard Philippe Groslier has also written on the art of Indo-China but has briefly touched upon the art style of Dong-duong. Majumdar's work is based on Parmentier and gives a general survey of the Cham art. H.B. Sarkar, George Coedés and other scholars have also touched upon this art style. J.C. Sharma, the former Indian Ambassador to Vietnam, has written a very insightful monograph on the living temples in the Chams area based on his personal visit and ground survey.[5]

According to Nicholas Tarling,[6] the archaeological remains of Dong-duong reveal a distinct art tradition. A number of artefacts

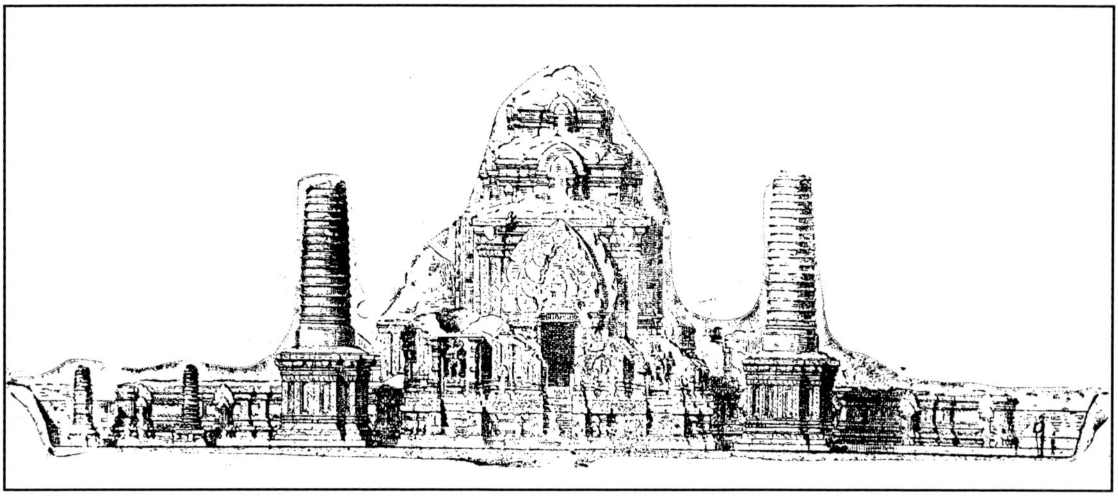

Pl. 5.1. Dong-duong temple (general view).

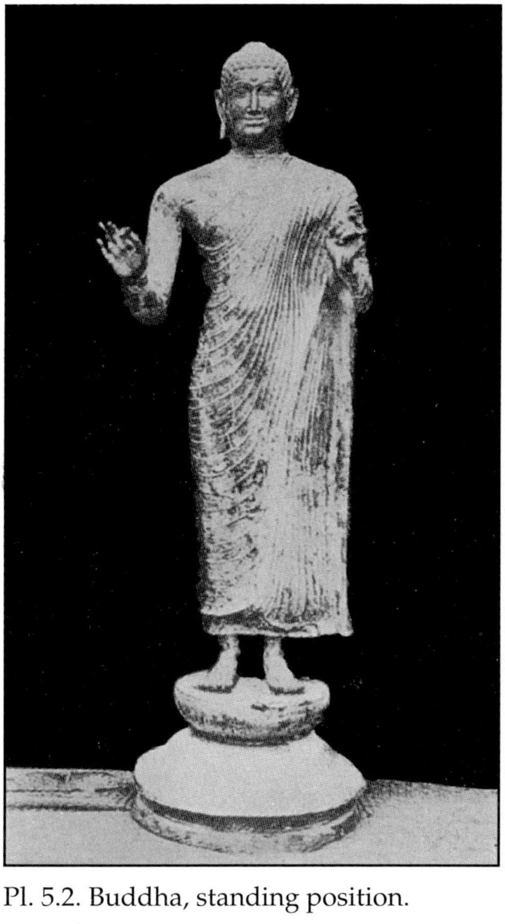

Pl. 5.2. Buddha, standing position.

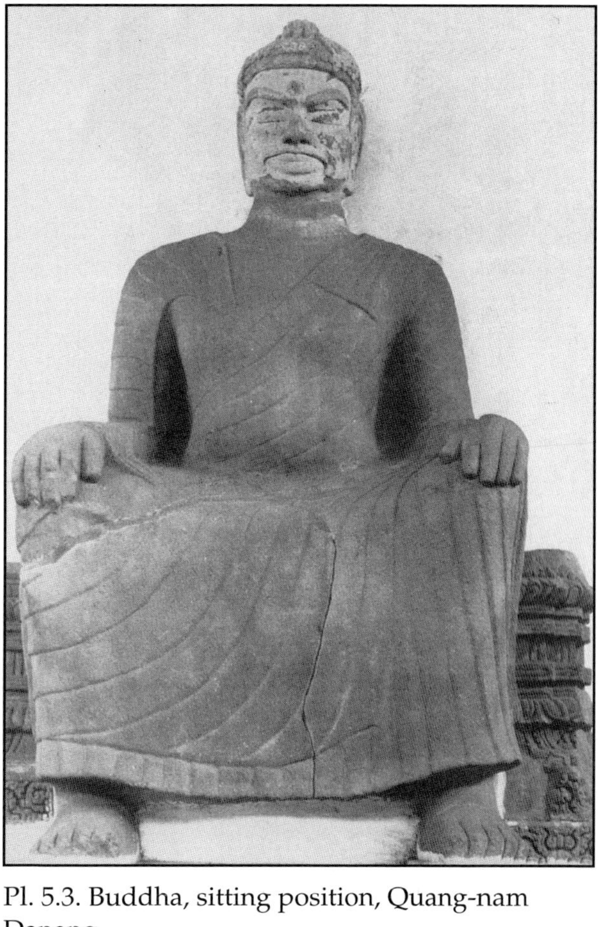

Pl. 5.3. Buddha, sitting position, Quang-nam Danang.

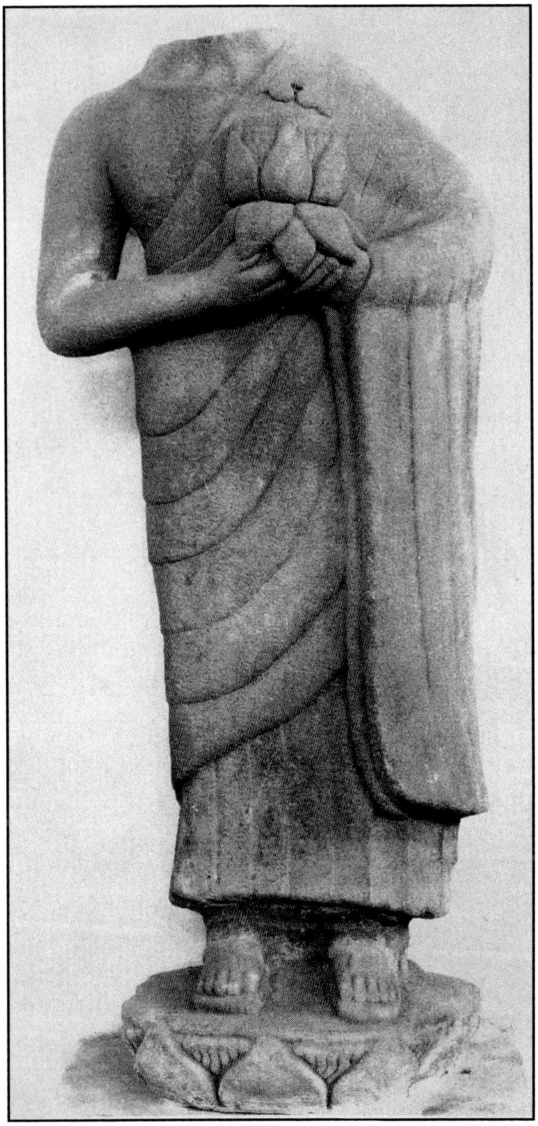

Pl. 5.4. Buddhist monk holding lotus in his hands, Quang-nam Danang.

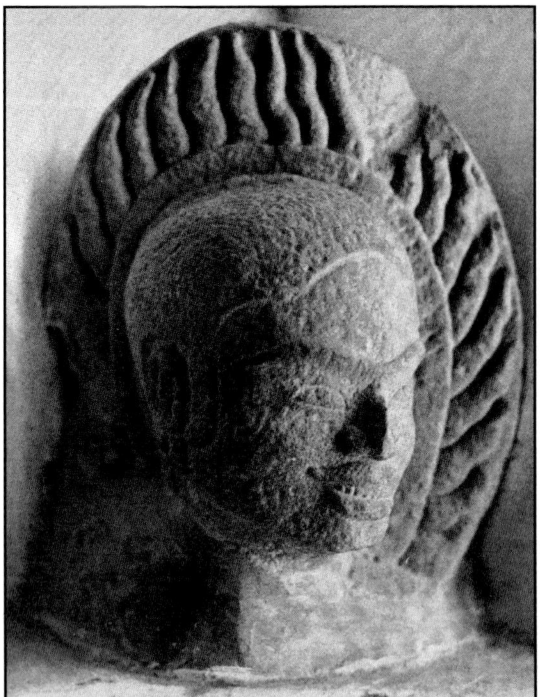

Pl. 5.5. Bodhisattva head, Quang-nam Danang.

unearthed, bear an imprint of Indian art style. Coedés identifies this place as a holy land of Chams. It seems plausible that religion was the main motivating force in the development of Dong-duong art style. The royal patronage played a significant role in its accomplishment.

Before analysing the Dong-duong art style, it is pertinent to throw some light on the promoters of this art style. The archaeological evidences reveal that this area was inhabited by the mighty Indianised Chams during the beginning of the Christian era. R.C. Majumdar opines that ethnically the Chams people originated from an Austronesian race.[7]

From the epigraphical records we learn that during the 9th century, Mahāyāna Buddhism was widely practised in Champa. Emperor Indravarman (AD 854-93) was a devout Buddhist. D.G.E. Hall mentions that the reign of Indravarman was peaceful and flourishing with a great Buddhist culture and splendid monasteries.[8]

The Chams were civilised people and had a rich cultural heritage as it appears from the Chinese text, named *Lin-yi-ki* of the end of the 5th century AD. The text mentions about the people of Kiu-sou (Chams) who had a fortified city about 70 miles away from the capital. The text also states that the Je-nan (Chinese exiled people) later came in contact with the local people (Chams). As a result of such contact, the traditional customs and manners of the Je-nan were completely transformed.[9]

## TEMPLE ARCHITECTURE

An impressive Buddhist (Pl. 5.1) temple at Dong-duong dedicated to Lakṣmindralokeśvara was constructed by Indravarman in AD 875. This Buddhist temple is also known as Dong-duong temple. It was the glorious period of Chams architecture. The ruins of the temple, about 12 miles to the south-east of Mi-son, cover a rectangular area 328 yards by 164 yards. It is enclosed by a low brick wall with only one opening to the east.

The rectangle is divided lengthwise in three long narrow blocks of slightly unequal dimensions running east to west. At the western end of the central block, is located the principal sanctuary X. It is surrounded by four sancturies built on the same terrace. An imposing building Y, with four bays, stands in front of X and there are two other temples P and Q and two residential blocks R and S. The complete structure is surrounded by a wall, forming the first courtyard. Along the sides of this wall, within the courtyard, are seven small temples. A porch in the eastern side of the wall serves as the only entrance to this courtyard. At the entrance of the porch are two columns more than 11 yards high.

To the east of Court I, there is Court II. It contains a long chamber and is likewise opened at the east end by a second porch preceded by two columns.

To the east of Court II, there is Court III. It contains an imposing hall opening to the east into a third porch preceded by two columns. There are two side entrances to the hall, one in the north and another in the south. It is followed by a number of long narrow courts, till one entered the fourth porch, which serves as the main entrance to the enclosure and is preceded by two columns.

The first court is flanked by two other on the north and south. The northern one contains the ruins of three temples, and the southern, those of a square chamber. These two side courts together with Court I, are surrounded by a wall. Similarly Court II is also surrounded by a wall of enclosure.

The south-eastern corner of the rectangular area is covered by ruins of brick buildings and the north-eastern corner by a hollow basin. The walls of Court II and Court III are decorated on the inner side. The long narrow passage, which connects the main gate with the principal temple in Court I, appears to be the only portion really built for the public.

Majumdar opines that the different buildings were possibly constructed in different ages extending the whole group gradually towards the east. It is just possible, however, that all these buildings were part of the original plan and at first made up of wood, being replaced at the later date by more durable materials.[10]

The principal temple which is located on the western end of the central block belongs to the normal type—but there are large niches in the interior and big projections in front of the false doorways on the exterior of the walls. The complete building thus appears in the cross-shape. In addition to the staircase in front, is the main doorway on the western side. Both are nicely carved and decorated with elegant figures. The false doorways are decorated with richly ornamented pilasters and beautiful statues. The walls of the courts are also decorated with pilasters and figures. In front of them are a series of ornamented brick columns, cylindrical in plan placed on a square block and are adorned by a series of rings. Sarkar[11] thinks that the construction plan of the Dong-duong temple reminds one of the layout of the Paharpur (U.P., India) brick temple.

## THE CAVE ART

The Chams were closely associated with the nature and in a simple and artistic style converted their natural places into shrines. They artistically decorated their natural caves without disturbing its natural beauty.

A nice natural cave is found in the province of Quang-nam Danang which has been turned to a Buddhist shrine. The decorative design of this cave is very simple. A beautiful Buddha image is installed on a natural rock. The natural beauty of this cave has not been touched.

## SCULPTURES AND ART STYLE

The art style of Dong-duong was fairly well developed as it appears from the description of Dong-duong inscription No. 36. It mentions that "the city named Champa was decorated with the wealth of Purindrapura. It was beautified by lotus tanks containing white lotus." The beauty was so elegant that none could surpass it.[12] Even to this day, the Dong-duong area contains tanks abounding in lotus. From the epigraphical evidence, we find more details about the beauty of the city. Dong-duong inscription no. 31 mentions that in the city, there were places where the images of Indra, Brahmā, Viṣṇu were installed. Images of Śiva (*Śaṅkara*), ascetics (*ṛṣis*), Sun, Moon, Varun, Fire (*Agni*), Abhayada (Buddha) were also placed in different parts of the city for the deliverance of the living beings.[13]

The Dong-duong sculptures, found in limited number, show its particular original art style while remaining integrated within Cham characters under the influence of Indian art. Two major characteristics have been noticed in this art style. One is that indigenous style bearing national character being fused with foreign art styles. Another is the folk style having serious facial expression along with elegant ornamental designs and floral motifs. The internationalisation of various art styles has mingled in such a way that sometimes it is very difficult for scholars to recognise other art styles.

The sculptors have very efficiently shown religious motifs in their art work. This art style reveals mainly Mahāyāna character. A large number of Buddha statues have been found in the archaeological ruins of Dong-duong. These images look imposingly sublime. The Buddha image of the Court III of Dong-duong temple reflects the features of Indian post-Gupta art style. It has folded dress, the *ūrṇā*, the *uṣṇīṣa* and arranged hairs. This statue expresses both serenity and dignity.

One of the images found from Dong-duong locality, is in a sitting posture (Pl. 5.3) with hands on the knees, the body and head in an erect position, the eyes looking straight forward. The fold of dress is symmetrical with curved lines. There is another image of Buddha in the sitting posture on a pedestal. The head of the image is missing. The pedestal consists of four layers. It has animal figures and is decorated by waivy design at the centre.

The best-known specimen of Dong-duong sculpture is a standing bronze Buddha image (Pl. 5.2) dressed in a pleated monastic robe. The arms are symmetrically folded but the figure has a rather unnatural look. This sculpture appears to be a prototype and bears resemblance to the Amarāvatī style[14] of the early centuries in the Christian era. Coedés opines that this image belongs to the Gupta style and dates it to the 4th century AD.[15] It is generally felt that the earliest South-East Asian Buddha figures have been directly inspired by the Anuradhpur style of Sri Lanka which bears a strong influence of Amarāvatī[16] and belong to the period between the 4th and 6th centuries AD.

This bronze Buddha image looks like Dīpaṇkar Buddha. During ancient times, the images of Dīpaṇkar Buddha were worshipped by the seamen. The seafaring people carried such images on board for their journey. Similar figures have also been found in the Korat area and Nakhon Pathom in Thailand and other parts of South-East Asia. The seamen of various places of South-East Asia still carry this image on board as a protector.

The Dong-duong inscription no. 31 (C-8) mentions that those who protect the gold, silver and metal wares of the Buddha will be reborn in the abode of the Buddha (i.e. in heaven). Even now, people of South-East Asia donate images of Buddha, protect the properties of monasteries and try to add to them. It seems quite plausible that a large number of images were casted for acquiring merits during ancient times and the Dong-duong Buddha image is one of the products of that period. However, there is no evidence to prove that this image was brought to Dong-duong immediately after it was made. Further research is required in this regard.

A fine headless sculpture of a Buddhist monk (Pl. 5.4) made in the late 9th century has also been found in the Dong-duong locality. It is beautifully sculpted. The monk's figure is holding an eight-petal lotus (*aṣṭadala kamala*). The robe is symmetrically pleated. The monk is wearing wooden slipper which is a rare sight. The pedestal of this image is a lotus. This sculpture typifies the originality and refinement of the art style. The influence of Indian art on Cham sculpture is clearly traceable in the decorative designs and motifs. For instance, the *padmā* (lotus) was a prominent motif in the art of Chams and as it was in the sculpture of Bharut, Sanchi and Amarāvatī.

*Padmā* is the emblem of purity and chastity. It grows from the dark watery mire but is untainted or unstained by it. As the lotus seed grows from the water and not from the earth's soil, it is the symbol of divinity, so it finds a place of pride in the religious sculptures. The lotus seat or throne on which most deities sit or stand symbolises their innate purity; they manifest into cyclic existence, yet they are completely free from its defilements, emotional hindrances and obscurations.

A sculpture dated late 9th century, of a Buddhist monk sitting in crossed-leg posture on *kamalāsana,* holding a musical instrument by both the hands has also been found in Dong-duong. The image's robe is pleated on the shoulder. The hair is curly. The musical instrument is very similar to the *dudumbhi* which is a common traditional musical instrument in India. It reveals the traditional indigenous features of Vietnam.

Groslier is of the view that the sculptures of Dong-duong reveal significant racial features. It can easily be noticed that the sculptures have thick lips, moustache, flat nose, heavy eyelid and thick joined eyebrows.[17] The Chinese account mentions that to the south and south-east beyond the Nanling mountains, there lived a large number of independent tribes who were not confined to Tonkin and the northern portion of Annam but spread as far as Quang-nam. These independent ethnic groups must have played an important role in the development of this art style.

A 9th century Buddha head (Pl. 5.5) with *prabhāmaṇḍala* has also been found from the Dong-duong area. The *prabhāmaṇḍala* is decorated with the wavey or flamy design. The face of the sculpture represents the tribal artistic features.

The Dong-duong inscription no. 31 (A-16) mentions that many religions were in practice in the cities of Champa. Besides Buddhism, Hinduism was popular in this area. A large number of adherents of the Śaivite cult were also inhabiting the area as revealed by the findings at La-tho (in the province of Quang-nam) and beautiful Śiva sculptures found from Dong-duong. From La-tho, we have a platter and a pitcher both inscribed in South Indian characters of a very early age, not later than the 6th century AD. The platter is made of an alloy in which silver predominates, and the inscription on it reads: Śrī Vanāntesvara. The pitcher is of silver and bears a *śloka*:

*Vanāntareśvarāyāsmai Śrīmate divayakīrttaye*
*Campāpirapatī raupyam kalaśam śraddhyātmanaḥ*[18]

(Here a king of Champa presenting silver vessels to a Śiva temple. The recorded Sanskrit verse is correct.)

The 0.7 metre high three-eyed stone sculpture of Lord Śiva (Pl. 5.6) sitting in a bending posture has been found. The style of the sculpture has similarity with the Avalokiteśvara posture. The god's head gear is a *kirīta-mukuṭa* which has floral design. The ear lobes are elongated wearing flower shaped long earrings which hang even beyond the shoulders. The neck has three prominent lines. A *dhoti* is tied around the waist. Behind the *kirīta-mukuṭa* is a *prabhāmandala* with a local decorative design. Here, Śaivite and Buddhist elements are reflected in this art style. Thus, Dong-duong art, sometimes reveals the synthesis of religious art. It also gives the impression of the co-existence of Śaivism and Buddhism.

Another image of Śiva, in a sitting position, has also been found. The deity's right hand is resting on the right bent knee while the left hand holds a vajra above the left leg which rests on the pedestal. Below the loin, the image is dressed in a sophistically designed cloth. The headgear is a trident shaped *kirīta-mukuṭa* which bears local decorative design. The elongated earlobes are with *karṇafula*, an Indian ornament.

The Rāmāyaṇa was very popular among the Chams. It is still preserved in the Annamite annals.[19] Episodes from the Rāmāyaṇa are seen in the Dong-duong relief. A relief on the pedestal shows multi-armed Dasanana (Rāvaṇa) (Pl. 5.7), the demon king, holding mountain Kailash, a symbolic site of Umā and Maheśvara (Śiva and his consort). The mountain is filled with stylised trident and stones. The pedestal appears to be a lotus flower. Upper portion of the pedestal has a beautiful design. Another beautiful piece is a relief of late 9th or early 10th century also featuring the Rāmāyaṇa episodes. The relief shows a monkey between two warriors. The two warriors could be identified as Rāma and Lakśmaṇa. The monkey would then be Hanumān. The monkey appears to be seeking the advice of Rāma while Lakśmaṇa looks on. A beautiful woman touching the artistic floral design adorns the beauty of the panel.

A beautiful pedestal of a congratulating deity has been found from Dong-duong. Here the deity is presented in half-human and half-fish form. The facial expression of the deity is quite ethnic. The nose and lips are broadened. There is another piece of sculpture, quite refined and unique. It is a warrior, probably a demon, emanating from a buffalo mouth. It seems to be an image of Mahīsāsūra.

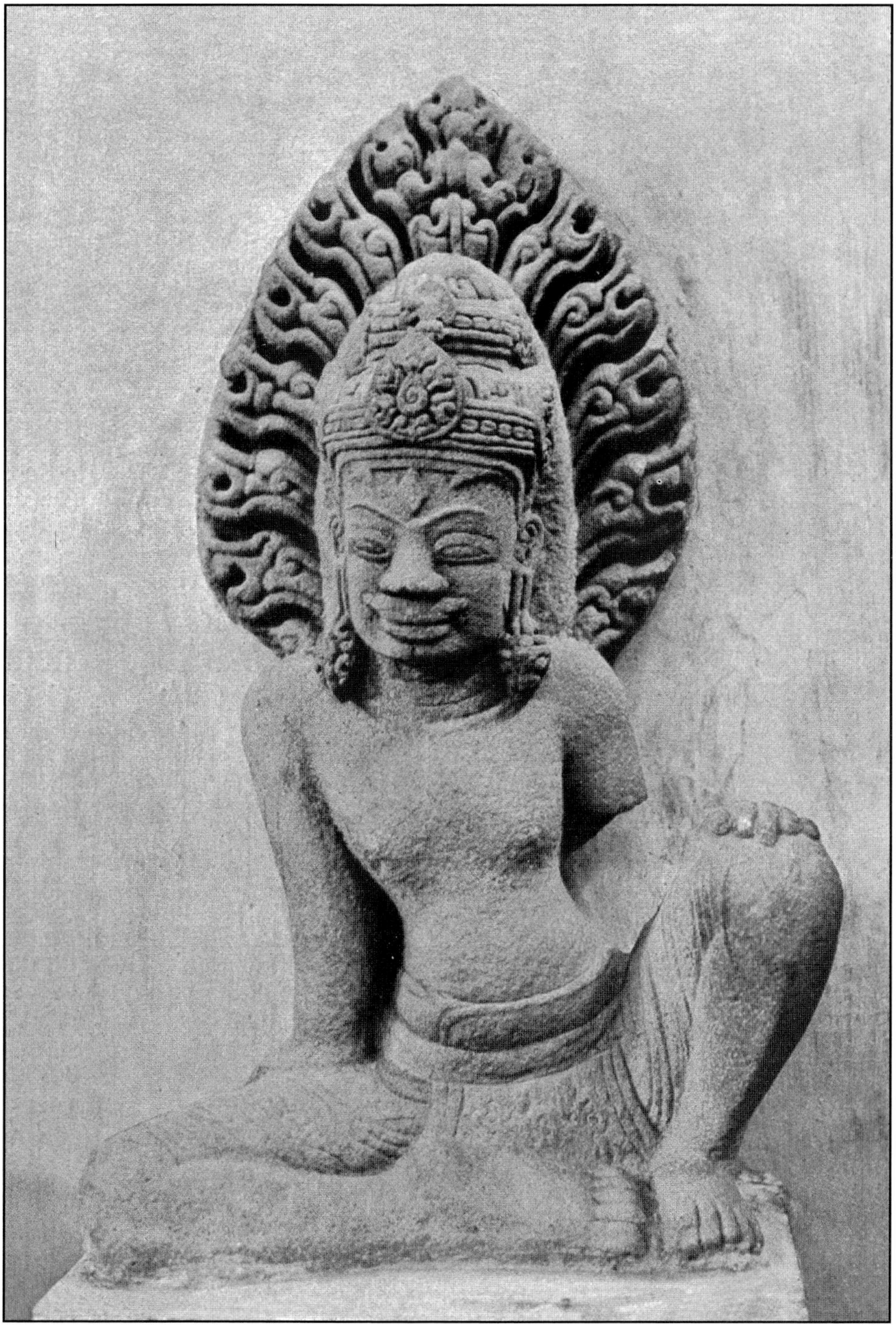

Pl. 5.6. Śiva, sitting position, Quang-nam Danang.

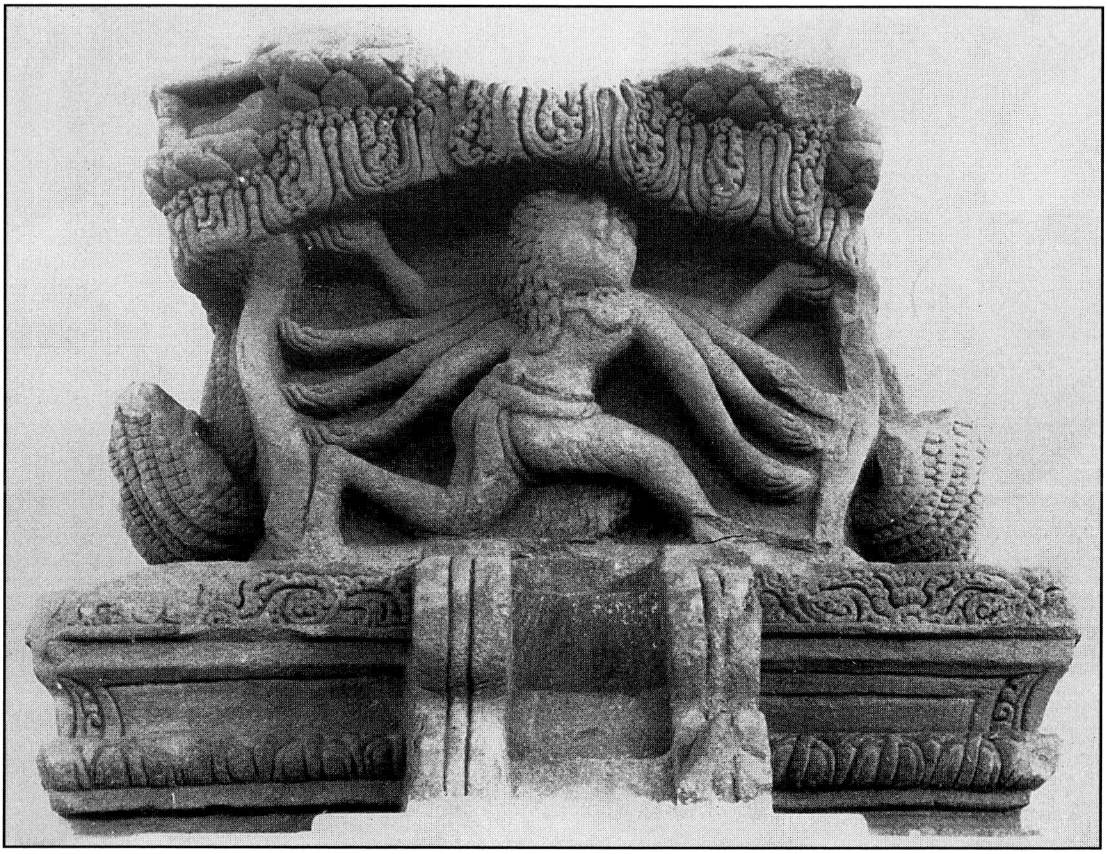

Pl. 5.7. Rāvaṇa having four pairs of hands lifting Kailash mountain, Quang-nam Danang.

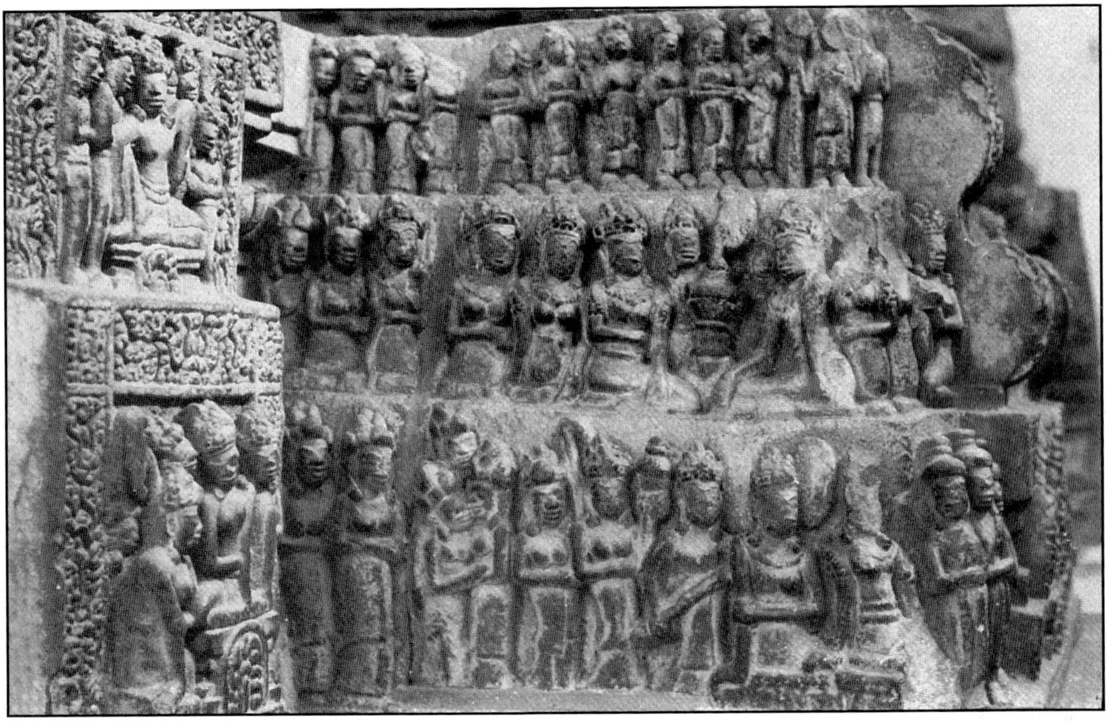

Pl. 5.8. Buddhist scenes, altar pedestal, Quang-nam Danang.

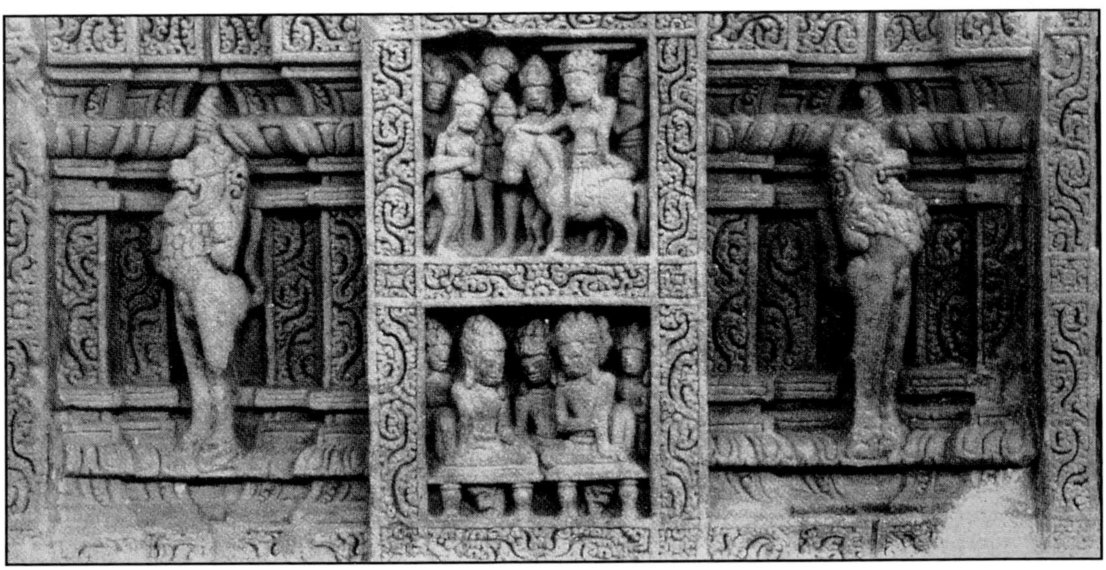

Pl. 5.9. Buddhist scenes, altar pedestal, Quang-nam Danang.

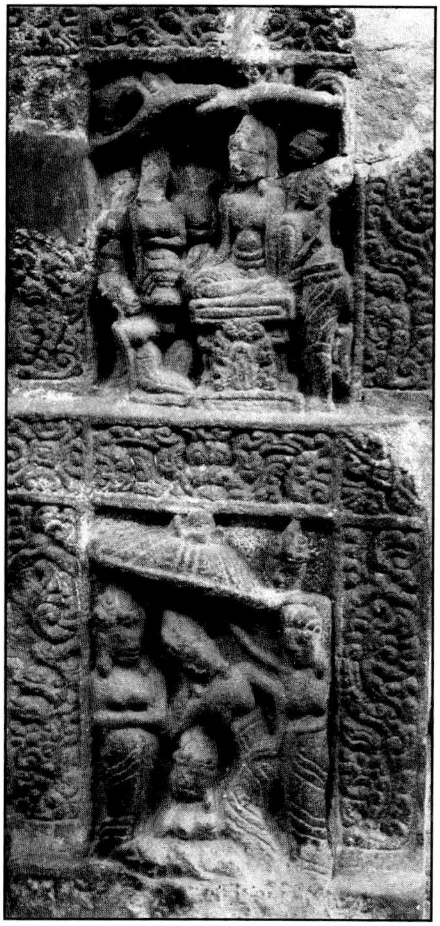

Pl. 5.10. Buddhist scenes, altar pedestal, Quang-nam Danang.

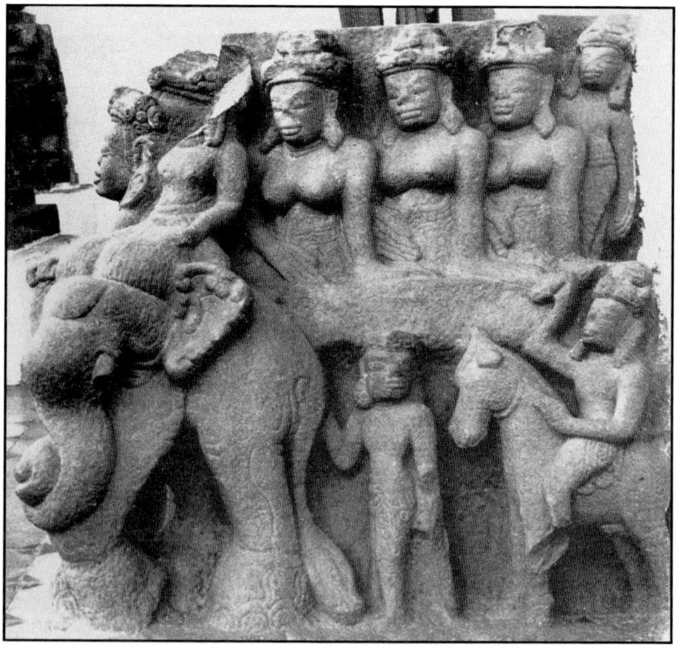

Pl. 5.11. On elephant, relief on altar base, Quang-nam Danang.

A large number of Buddhist panels have also been found from the premises of Dong-duong temple. A beautiful panel depicts a Buddhist scene (Pl. 5.10). The upper portion of the panel shows Lord Buddha in a sitting posture under the Bodhi tree along with six women attendants. The lower portion has the figures of three women. The middle one appears to be a queen bending towards the right under an umbrella. The bending posture resembles South Indian art style which is very common in Cham and Kḥmer art.

A beautiful altar pedestal depicting two Buddhist scenes (Pl. 5.9) has been found from Dong-duong locality. It has an intricate floral design. Besides, there is a beautifully executed lion. It resembles the early phase of Indian art. Another altar pedestal depicting Buddhist scene has been reported from the Dong-duong temple area. The figure appears to be a queen sitting on the elephant (Pl. 5.11) along with her attendants. A horse-rider is in command of the elephant.

The images of the door guardian have also been reported. There is a beautiful specimen of *dvarapāla* standing on an animal, probably an elephant. The most astonishing sculpture, found in the Dong-duong temple area, is a Śiva featuring as a *dvarapāla* in sitting posture.

The tympanum of the principal temple of Dong-duong depicts a large group of figures (Pl. 5.8), without making any distinction between principal and subsidiary ones. It contains about 40 seated figures divided into four or five panels—but they are too imperfectly engraved to give any clear ideas.[20]

The bas-reliefs on the pedestals of Dong-duong are richer in composition though of less artistic merit. They depict various scenes of war, processions, etc. and a large number of human figures of various statues. Their style resembles the art of Borobudur. It was probably due to a cultural dialogue between Champa and Java during 8th century. There was also a special trade partnership between the two lands lasting till 10th century. An inscription dated AD 911 records the adventure of Chams courtier, Rājadvāra. Rājadvāra twice travelled to Java to study Buddhist magic sciences, the word used for it is *siddhayātra* in the epigraphical record.

## ORNAMENTAL DECORATIONS

The Dong-duong art is enriched by floral decorations, injecting life to every shape and every detail. The Chams artists excelled in floral decorations. Although they treated foliage in a conventional manner, they added an element of grace and beauty which made it highly charming. The panels of Dong-duong are rich in wormlike patterns mixed with hooks and leftward and rightward spirals create a decorative style. The fig-leaf-form flowers are also used widely in the decoration of statues. Groslier[21] thinks that Chinese influence can be easily recognised in the decorative motifs. He links the s-shaped rows of crotchets with the pattern on Chinese bronzes.

The Chams were well acquainted with the Indian model of decorations. The lotus design which forms such a beautiful element in Indian art also figures largely in Dong-duong art.

## CONCLUSION

The Dong-duong art has a distinct feature, evolved under the royal patronage. It represents the amalgamation of Indian, Javanese and Khmer art elements but the style appears to be quite indigenous. However, the Indian art style is easily perceptible. Religious motifs dominated in this art style. Because of it, the aesthetic sense of the artists did not reflect much in this art style. The decorative style is superb and quite unique. The Chinese influence is also traceable. This style of art blossomed into full flower during late 9th and early 10th centuries which is regarded as the golden age of Vietnamese art. M. Parmentier, however, prefers to work on Chams rather than those originally from India as it is a purer work of art.

## NOTES AND REFERENCES

1. K.A. Nilakanta Sastri, *South Indian Influence in the Far East*, Bombay, 1949, p. 53.
2. George Coedés, *Indianized States of Southeast Asia*, Honolulu, 1968, p. 43.
3. R.C. Majumdar, *Champa: History and Culture of an Indian Colonial Kingdom in the Far East—2nd-16th Centuries A.D.*, reprint, Delhi, 1985, p. 102.
4. H. Paramentier, *Inventaire Descriptif des Monuments Chams De I'Annam*, Paris, 1909.
5. J.C. Sharma, *Hindu Temples in Vietnam*, New Delhi, 1997.
6. Nicholas Tarling, *The Cambridge History of South-East Asia* (from early times to *c.* 1800), I, Cambridge University Press, 1992, pp. 154-55.
7. R.C. Majumdar, *op. cit.*, p. 11.
8. D.G.E. Hall, *A History of South-East Asia*, New York, 1970, p. 186.
9. *BEFEO*, IV/9, p. 13.
10. R.C. Majumdar, *op. cit.*, pp. 249-50.
11. H.B. Sarkar, *Cultural Relations Between India and South-East Asian Countries*, 1985, p. 335.
12. R.C. Majumdar, *op. cit.*, p. 102.

13. *Ibid.*, p. 86.
14. Virgile Rougier, "Nouvelles Decouvertes Chams au Quang-nam", *BCAI,* 1912, pp. 212-13; Ananda K. Coomaraswamy, *History of Indian and Indonesian Art*, New York, 1927, p. 197.
15. George Coedés, *op. cit.,* Singapore edition, 1968, pp. 17-18, 49.
16. Nicholas Tarling, *op. cit.*, p. 291.
17. B.P. Groslier, *Indochina: Art in the Melting-pot of Races,* London, 1962, p. 141.
18. *BCAI,* 1912, pl. ix, pp. 211-12; *BEFEO,* xi, figs. 42, 43, pp. 471-72; as reconstructed Vol. xxi, pl. xi. The verse is also quoted in K.A. Nilakanta Sastri, *op. cit.,* pp. 53-54,
19. R.C. Majumdar, *op. cit.,* p. 13.
20. H. Parmentier, *op. cit.,* p. 470, fig. 104.
21. B.P. Groslier, *op. cit.,* p. 141.

# 6

# The Art of Vietnam and Cambodia: An Overview

Lokesh Chandra

From the point of view of art history, Vietnam and Cambodia are quite distinct. Putting them together is partly due to geographic contiguity but perhaps more so because they formed spheres of French domination. For appropriate scientific studies, this clubbing has to be abandoned as the two countries have clear-cut cultural identities. Indo-China came into being in 1887. Within a short span of about sixty years, European scholars found the distinct cultural personalities of Vietnam, Cambodia, Laos and contiguous Thailand. Vietnam is a Chinese expression. Viet is the Annamite pronunciation of Chinese *Yueh,* which means 'wild'. It means the 'Wild South'. The culturisation of Vietnam revolves around coastline Indo-China and inland Indo-China. Coastline Indo-China had quadrangular adze from the Neolithic period which also prevailed in Indonesia. The connection of coastline Indo-China to Indonesia was close. Inland Indo-China was related, culturally and from the point of view of material civilisation, with the Chinese lenticular adze as early as the Neolithic period. Coastline Indo-China had a distinct personality in history, governed by the Chams under the name of Champa, from the Indian kingdom of Champa on the eastern coast. Founded by the Cham people in AD 192, Champa disappeared in the 17th century. The first dynasty of Champa was of Indian origin, while the second dynasty was founded in AD 336 by a fugitive Chinese slave. From the 5th century onwards when the sacred city of temples was built at Siṃhapura, Champa was Śaiva. Vietnam was known as Tonkin, Annam and Cochin China during the French period. Tonkin was the northern part, with Hanoi as its major city. Annam means the 'Pacified South'. It was the central part of Vietnam with the metropolitan city of Hue. Close to Hue are the Cham temples of Śiva. The southernmost part of Vietnam was known as Cochin China or Nam Bo, with its capital at Saigon. These distinctive parts of Vietnam have to be borne in mind when cultural evolution is taken into consideration.

Vietnamese art shows predominance of the Chinese idiom and Annamese has been treated as a Chinese dialect in the classical Chinese dictionary of Herbert A. Giles. Three chronological periods of culture can be distinguished in Vietnam. The first is the Bronze Age, the Dongson period (4th century BC to the 1st century AD). The second period lasted from the 1st to the 10th century of the Christian era, and Chinese dominated the scene. Funerary architecture of this period, with materials from the tombs, is through and through Chinese. There are Buddhist statues of Lokapālas, Kinnaras, Vajrapāṇi and so on. This Buddhist art of Vietnam has rarely been studied. A general work on it deserves to be taken up with the collaboration of experts in Vietnam and India, as well as in Japan, China and Europe. From the 10th to the 13th centuries Vietnam was Sino-Vietnamese. After the 13th century Vietnamese art emerged gradually. From the 13th century up to the present day, a distinct Vietnamese idiom of art has evolved. A number of *stūpas* have survived from the 11th century onwards but they have to be studied, and to have easy access to them they have to be photographed. Detailed photographic documentation of these *stūpas* from the point of view of the art historian, and historian of architecture would be a historic step in the study of Vietnamese culture. It will provide a rich source for understanding the evolution of the Buddhist art of Vietnam, for example, Binh-son stūpa (11-12th century), Kao-phien stūpa (1057), Ly Nhon-ton stūpa (1121), Pho-minh stūpa. The Thien-phuc temple (1132) has Cham motifs, like the Garuḍa. From the 12th century onwards, influences from Java can also be seen, probably through Champa. All these elements have always been overlooked and they constitute a major field where Indians can contribute, besides the restoration of these monuments.

For the last hundred years the French have written on them. They have done stupendous studies, which will not be repeated. We will have to build on the infrastructures created by them, as well as add new visions and facts. R.C. Majumdar summarized the classics of French scholarship into English. We have to read French to study the culture of Vietnam.

Cambodia came into prominence when Henri Mouhot wrote about the ruins of Angkor in 1860. His work remains a classic as a sensitive and inspiring approach to the monuments of Cambodia. Though antiquated, it provides the psychosphere whence emerged the study of the culture of Cambodia. About five hundred years ago, a Japanese monk went to the monuments in Angkor in search of Gandhāra. He felt that he had arrived in Gandhāra and he has bequeathed his drawings and sketches of the Angkor Wat. Some of these sketches are valuable, as a number of things have disappeared or details have got blurred with the passage of time and by erosion due to the inclemency of the monsoon rains. The provinces of Siem Reap and Battambang were restored to Cambodia by the treaty of 23rd March 1907. Thereafter, French scholars took an active interest in the restoration of Angkor. They were taken up by the idea of the centre. They called it the temple mountain, mountain-temple, or the pyramidal temple. In fact, it is the Sumeru with the Sudarśana palace of Devarāja Indra. The Sumeru is an important concept of architecture and consecration of the kingdom-state. The terminology surrounding Sumeru and Devarāja is crucial to the understanding of Cambodia's history. The deified images of royal ancestors begin with the inscriptions of Mūlavarman from Kalimantan in Indonesia. The hydraulic works for irrigation are referred to as Jaladhenu in an inscription of Mūlavarman. Besides, roads, inns, hospitals and other public-utility works constituted *pūrtadharma* for the king. The sociology of the Khmer state deserves a closer study.

The evolution of the Cambodian art can be classified as pre-Angkorian, Angkorian and post-Angkorian. Pre-Angkorian art has three distinct phases: (i) Funan from the end of the 6th to the beginning of the 7th century. The images are characterised by frontality and *tribhaṅga*. The oldest image is that of Harihara from Asram Maharosei. (ii) The second phase of Sambor lasted for a short span of the first half of the 7th century. The portrait statues are marked by grandeur and serenity, dignity and vitality, without insistence on details. (iii) The third phase is Prei Khmeng and Kompong Prah.

Angkorian art began in the 9th century and endured for five centuries. The first phase lasted from the 9th to the 11th centuries. It began with King Jayavarman II who seized power and proclaimed independence from Java *c.* AD 802. About 700 centres have been identified around ancient capitals. The second phase commenced with Sūryavarman I. It is the golden age of Khmer art whose crowning glory is Angkor Wat. Post-Angkorian art survives to the present with its costumes, ornaments, coiffure in paintings and performing arts. The work of Madeleine Giteau on post-Angkorian iconography, published from Paris in 1975 is an eye-opener. If we want to achieve a breakthrough, the French classics on Vietnam and Cambodia have to be translated, so that detailed work can be undertaken. The post-Angkorian system is a living tradition in Kambuja. To understand this living tradition and its relationship to the classical art of the Angkorian period, it is essential to translate the work of Madame Giteau.

India has linguistic capabilities for original work through Sanskrit texts, by relating them to the monuments and through the interpretation of Cambodian inscriptions in Sanskrit. The translations of George Coedés, though of great pioneering value, are in need of revision as new source-materials have been made available since Coedés wrote.

I am happy that the Indira Gandhi National Centre for the Arts has taken the initiative to study the civilisations of these countries, with which we had and have cultural relations. To India they were 'Islands of Gold' or *Suvarṇadvīpa. Suvarṇadvīpa* is not only Sumatra nor only Java but connotes the several islands and lands of affluence in South-East Asia. Today they are *Suvarṇadvīpas* or golden isles of culture.

# 7

# Apsarās at Angkor Wat

K.M. Srivastava

A dreamland of fabulous and fascinating monuments, Cambodia has been a centre of magnetic attraction to art historians, tourists and general visitors from all over the world alike right through the ages. Lost completely in the thick of forests and completely unknown to the world until the later part of the 19th century, the monuments of Cambodia are the mute witnesses of the prosperous and glorious days of the Khmer emperors, who wrought their dreams into magnificent stone temples—marvels of sculptures and ornamentation. The monuments, with their extent, magnitude and splendour, dwarved and reduced almost to common place, the much heralded wonders located in any corner of the earth. They spell out clearly the genius of the Khmer civilisation, which reached its zenith during the 12th century AD. Of the large number of monuments, each distinctive in its own way, the temple of Angkor Wat (Pl. 7.1) in greyish sandstone is easily singled out as the most precious example in the Angkor region. Angkor Wat is located in north-western Cambodia just to the north of the small but brisk modern town of Siem Reap. The city of Angkor in ancient times served as the royal centre, wherefrom the Khmer kings ruled one of the largest, most prosperous and sophisticated kingdoms in the history of South-East Asia. Cambodia is situated between 103.10° and 106.55° East and 10.50° and 14.10° North.

Setting a singular example in world history, the Khmer kingdom of Cambodia endured a strange sequence of quick rise and fall, prosperity and chaos, followed by rapid changes in the dynasty and religious faith of the kings, almost like tidal waves. Greatly influenced by Indian culture, the history of Cambodia had a very early beginning (Gupta dynasty of India appearing about AD 320) and though there were more than thirty rulers in quick succession, three of them, among a dozen, who ruled at Angkor, occupy an outstanding position. They are Yaśovarman I (AD 889-900), Sūryavarman II (AD 1113-50) and Jayavarman VII (AD 1181-1219), worshippers respectively of Śiva, Viṣṇu and Buddha. Their faith, however, was not so much a devotion, but a source of power bestowed by the gods. Through a new cult of the *devarāja* (*deva,* god; *rājā,* ruler), or god-king, the ruler derived his sanctity and power. The *liṅga* (the phallic form of Śiva's creative force) had been designated as the *devarāja* by Jayavarman II in AD 802. The concept of divine royalty was spelt out in Khmer inscriptions as *Kamrateng Jagat ta raja,* or lord of the world who is king.

The three emperors, mentioned in conjunction above all, concentrated their building activity at Angkor, the exact meaning of which in Sanskrit is city from the word *nokor*. Angkor was sacked by the Thais in AD 1431 and this forced the Khmers to abandon the place. The monuments were thereafter left to the mercies of nature, the result of which has been dramatically described by Malcolm MacDonald in a single sentence.

> The man-borne woods of Dunsinane did not advance more rapidly and inexorably on Macbeth than the jungle of Cambodia marched on Angkor.[1]

Except for occasional references to the Angkor ruins, the monuments and the great civilisation that they represented were completely lost to the world. It was not until 1860 that they were once again brought to light by a French naturalist, Henry Mouhot, who noticed the grey towers of Angkor Wat through the gaps in the foliage. To quote MacDonald once again,

> Coming upon Angkor amid rustic and jungled Cambodia—the Cambodia of a century ago—was like being suddenly transported from barbarism to civilisation, from profound darkness to light.[2]

The monuments were made known to the world by the diary of Henri Mouhot, which was published posthumously in 1864.

Amongst all the emperors, who ruled at Angkor, Sūryavarman II (AD 1113-50) will remain immortal in the annals of history for constructing the temple of Angkor Wat, dedicated to Viṣṇu. In the 12th century, a strong wave of Viṣṇu worship swept South-East Asian countries, and under its influence Sūryavarman II became a devotee. Thus the exploits of Viṣṇu are depicted in almost every part of the temple, which was built to represent symbolically Mount Meru, traditionally regarded as Viṣṇu's abode. It stands out as a masterpiece of classical Khmer art, both in massiveness and ornamental details—the ultimate expression of all the grouping, growth and elaboration of religious architecture by the Khmer kings through the centuries. The temple of Angkor Wat shows clearly that the artists in their service possessed a sound knowledge of stereometry, without which the creation of a perfect step pyramid would not have been possible. The rise of the terraces is so well-calculated that they all appear to be of equal height, without obscuring the view of other terraces. A perfect harmony of proportion is also displayed in the balance between vertical and horizontal plains.

Artists chiselled virtually the entire surface of the temple of Angkor Wat with a variety of decorations. Some areas wear only a light overall design, which is so delicate that one has almost to feel it with his hands to know that it is there. Floral, human and animal depiction incorporated in the traceries are so minute that one has to stare at them to observe their presence. Elsewhere the decorations burst forth with lively vigour. They depict a variety of subjects like the eternal battles between gods and demons, spear-hurling warriors on chariots driven by horses and clawing monkeys. The theme of these dramatic scenes is drawn form Indian holy texts and the ancient classic epics, the Rāmāyaṇa and the Mahābhārata, which King Sūryavarman II might have chosen as symbols of his own life and deification. With Rāma and Kṛṣṇa incarnations, Vaiṣṇava themes occupy an upper hand in the narrative of the bas-reliefs. In order to exhibit his own martial spirit and inculcation of faith, Sūryavarman II selected the battlefield of Kurukshetra with Kṛṣṇa and Arjun in the forefront to catch the first attention of the people. Eleven episodes from the Rāmāyaṇa in all (including the pursuit of the golden deer by Rāma, the duel of Bali and Sugriva and final fire ordeal of Sīta), five exploits of Kṛṣṇa (including the breaking of the twin trees and lifting of the Govardhana hill), four scenes of Viṣṇu lore (including his Seshasayi form) and three scenes of Śaiva lore (including the burning of the god of love by Śiva and Rāvaṇa shaking the Kailāśa mountain) find a place in the carvings of the bas-reliefs. In the eastern gallery, the gods and the demons are shown trying their strength at the multiple-headed *naga,* churning of the sea (Pl. 7.2) thereby for bringing out the *amṛta.* Beginning with the court of Yama (god of death and justice), the panel of the Day of Judgement is the most intriguing tableaux of Angkor Wat. The saintly figures rise to occupy exalted pavilions. The evils are driven into thirty-two hells to such tortures as having their bones broken, being thrust

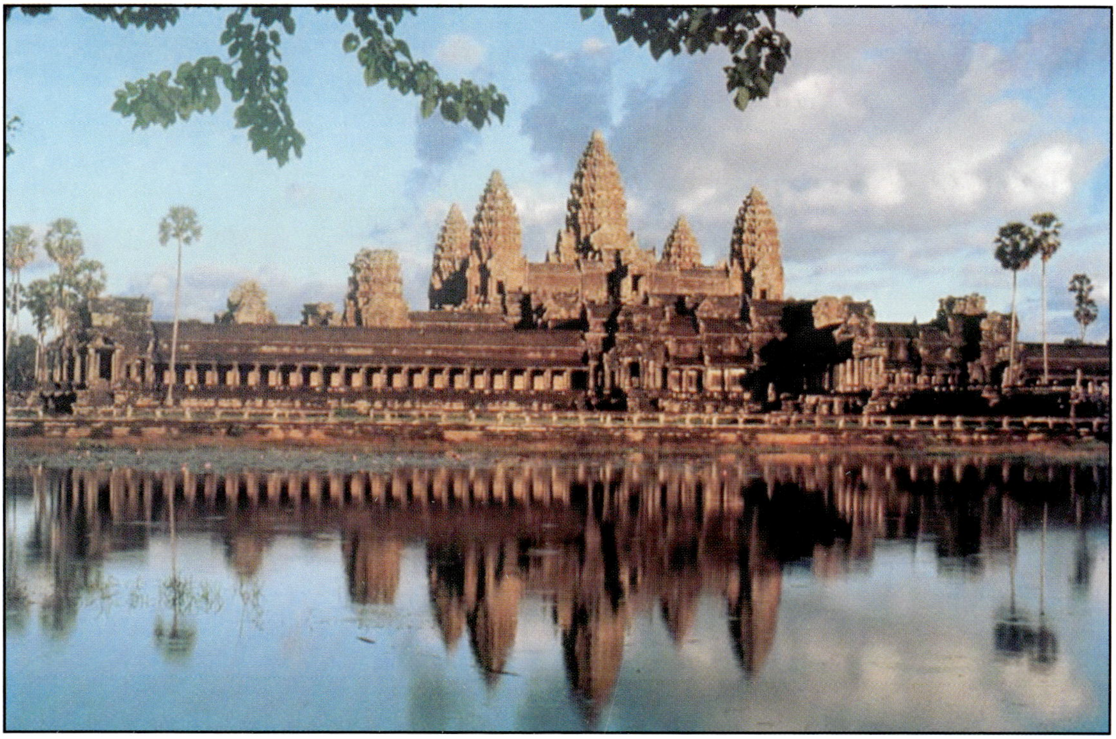

Pl. 7.1. Angkor Wat (general view).

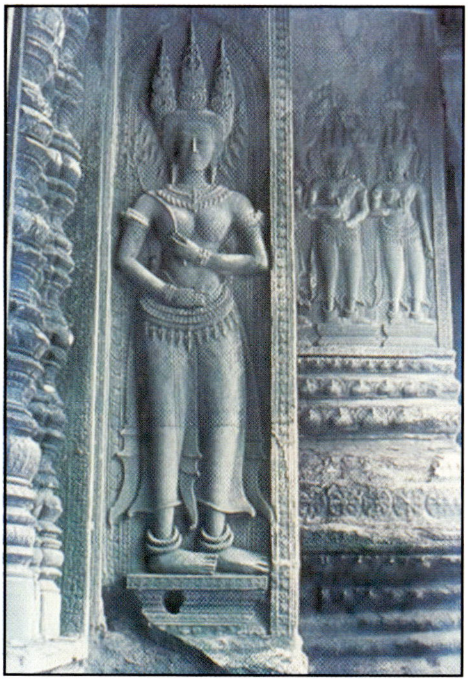

Pl. 7.3. Single *apsarā* with a group of two *apsarās* at Angkor Wat.

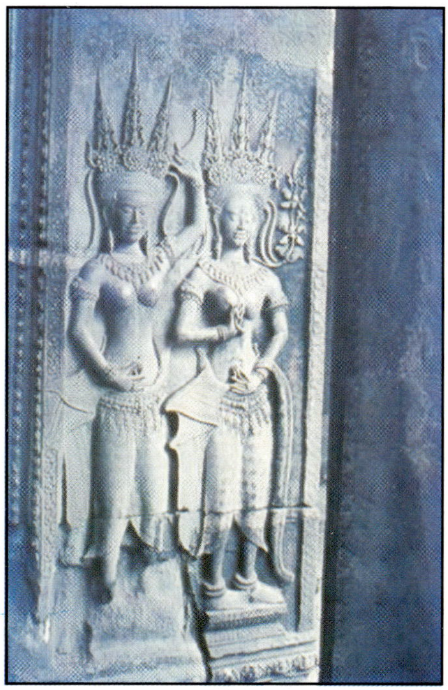

Pl. 7.4. A pair of *apsarās* at Angkor Wat.

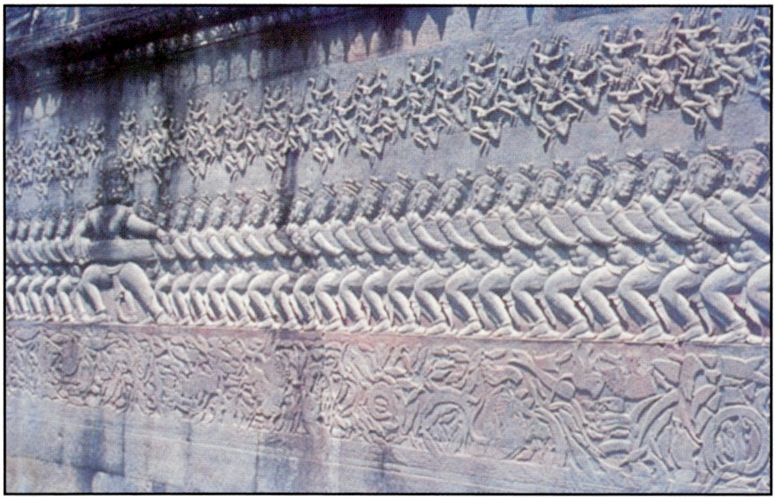

Pl. 7.2. Panel at Angkor Wat showing episode of *Samudra Manthan* (churning of the ocean).

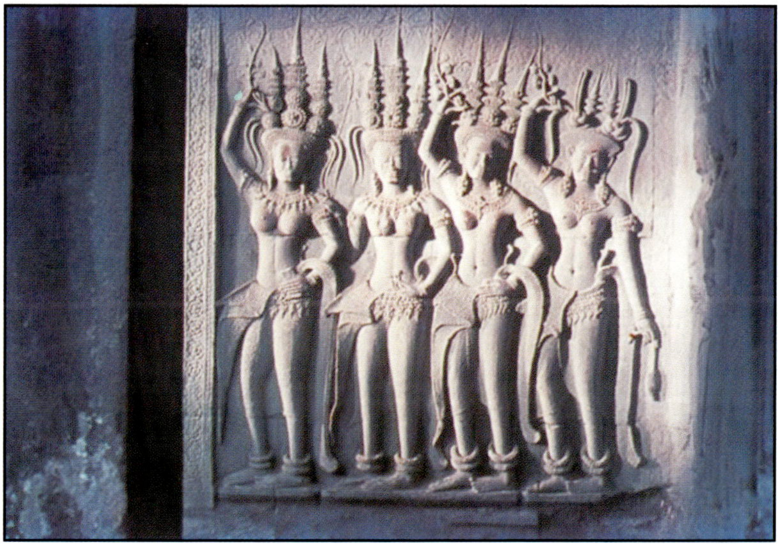

Pl. 7.5. A group of four *apsarās* at Angkor Wat.

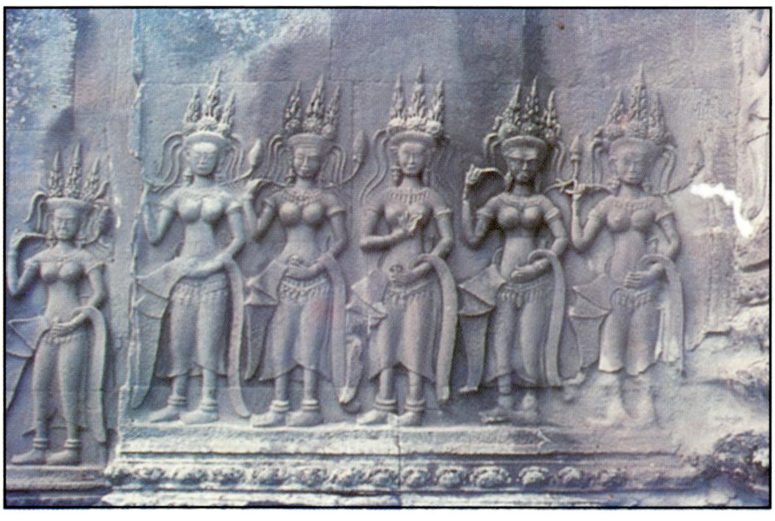

Pl. 7.6. A group of six *apsarās* at Angkor Wat.

into boiling pots, pinioned on racks, or cast to wild beasts. The name of each hell has been inscribed in Khmer language and the torture of sinners portrayed with blood-curdling vivacity. Of all, the most impressive in the bas-reliefs are the two portraits of Sūryavarman II.

The personal appearance of the king has been majestically portrayed with jewelled crown, heavy earrings, ornate necklace, a bracelet on each arm and wrist, and an ornamental belt with dangling sword. As many as fourteen umbrellas, four fly-whisks and five large fans distinguish the king, while he occupies the throne in a graceful manner. In pomp and show, he is in no way behind the Indian kings. The members of the Cabinet can be observed with the king, the designation of each having been mentioned below the figures. With the ministers the king is also seen with helmeted armed chiefs of the army. The king rides with his lords in an imposing state procession. An accoutred general on an elephant, with four horsemen before him, like outsiders, is followed by another distinguished person on an elephant, two footmen carrying the figures of Garuḍa and Hanumān and half a dozen more men. They are all marching before the king, who is accoutred and stands on his elephant, which bears on his head a diadem. Following further are two chiefs and a palanquin in which the royal priest is seated. Behind it is a group of priests carrying the sacred fire in an ark. Entirely different from the processions all over the world, the Cambodian procession has its musicians in the rear. The royal band consists of trumpet, conch and cymbal. Accompanying the band, two buffoons walk in dancing gait.

Of all the ornamentation in the temple of Angkor Wat, *apsarās*, the embodiments of beauty, in every nook and corner of the temple and more than sixteen hundred in number occupy the most important position. Appreciating the depiction of celestial nymphs Wilbur E. Garrett commented, "For eight centuries this serene and seductive celestial dancer has graced the entrance to the temple of Angkor Wat, holding promise of the imagined delights of the heaven." Aged yet ageless, she represents, in the Khmer lore of the 12th century, "the one who goes through the water of the clouds." Throughout the great religious complex at Angkor, thousands of these delicately carved *apsarās* bear witness to the glories of the Khmer empire that ruled Indo-China for six centuries. Time mellowed her lines but left her beauty undiminished.[3]

*Apsarās* are the celestial nymphs who symbolise the waters of heaven or the energy of ocean. The word *apsarās* is explained as *apsu rasa,* i.e. the essence of ocean water produced at the Churning, when *apsarās* and the physician god Dhanvantri first rose from it. According to *Puranic Encyclopaedia,* "An *apsarā* is a nymph (*devastrī*). These women were born at the time of the Churning of the Ocean of Milk."[4] "The *apsarās*", as stated by Cunningham, "were divine nymphs who were said to have sprung from the Churning of the Ocean. They were as famous for their skilful singing and dancing as for their beauty."[5] Gopinath Rao is also of the same opinion when he said, "the *apsarās* are so called because they are said to have sprung from the waters when the ocean was churned for obtaining ambrosia (*amṛta*)."[6] Those born out of the elements of ocean (associated with Brahman—the Creator) are *apsarās.* The phenomenal world was engrossed in the beginning in an unmanifested energy of ocean designated as Aditi in Vedic terms. The *apsarās* are born out of that ocean. The ultimate reality is that before the birth of the phenomenal world, there was a mighty ocean, which was the source of the vast element of motherhood. In Purāṇas, the same element has been christened as Dakṣa. Various manifestations of the element of motherhood owe their birth to the same Dakṣa and in consequence are called the daughters of Dakṣa, known as *apsarās*. In this way, the element of motherhood in various forms, born out of the element of ocean in the phenomenal world, is known as *apsarās*. Goldstücker has furnished a graphic and detailed account of *apsarās* in his Sanskrit dictionary. "As regards their origin", he states, "the Rāmāyaṇa makes them arise from the ocean, when it was churned by the gods for obtaining *amṛta*"[7] In the last mythological epoch, when the Gandharvas have been saved from their elementary nature merely so much as to be the musician in the paradise of Indra, the *apsarās* appear, among other subordinate deities which share in the "merry life of Indra's heaven", as the wives of the Gandharvas, but more specially as "wives of a licentious sort"; and they are promised as a reward as well to heroes fallen in battle, when they are received into the paradise of Indra. Indian literature is replete with a large number of references to *apsarās* right from the times of *Ṛgveda* till 12th century AD.

To a modern man of India, the kings, as well as their court-poets who composed the laudatory verses for copper-plates and inscriptions, appear to be indecent. They take pride not only in capturing the women of defeated countries but also in openly proclaiming before the world their dalliance with them. Sexual desire was always treated as one of the important instincts of life, hence its satisfaction was regarded as being as essential as any other duty. Gods and goddesses enjoyed sex as much as the human mortals. The only difference between a common man and a god was the designation of a woman; in the case of a common man they were known as prostitutes, whereas the partners of the gods were called *apsarās*. Love as *kāma* (sexuality) has been identified as the first seed of the cosmic mind in the hymns of the *Ṛgveda* in India and as such deified. As one of the important things in life, sex has, therefore, been freely depicted in Indian literature and art. Angkor was in a large measure a product of Indian influence on the indigenous Khmer society. The blending of the indigenous society, with the foreign Indian culture led to the development of a distinctive Khmer art.

Though the title of *devarāja* was assumed by Jayavarman II in the year AD 802, the institution of *apsarās* appears to have come into existence at a much later date. They were apparently first carved in the temples during the reign of Yaśovarman I, who is said to have laid the foundation of the capital Phnom Bakheng in Angkor in AD 889. The name of the capital in the initial stages was Kambujapuri, which was changed to Yaśodarapura at a later date. Yaśovarman I (AD 889-900) can, therefore, be considered as the founder of Angkor and its civilisation. The foundations for the glorious period of Kambuja were in fact laid by Indravarman I in AD 877, but they were consolidated by powerful kings like Yaśovarman I and Rājendravarman (AD 944-68) under whom there was a considerable expansion of the dominion of the empire. The *apsarās* at Phnom Bakheng are rather squat and plump and their bodily proportions are also not perfect.

Of the many structures raised by Rājendravarman, the most remarkable and attractive one was the temple of Banteay Srei, meaning Citadel of the Woman. It stands at an isolated place about 30 km from Angkor and was built in the last year of Rājendravarman's reign. In the charming temple of Banteay Srei, the *apsarās* appear in great contrast to the ones at Phnom Bakheng, so far as their elasticity, glamour and superb feminine beauty leading to great sexual appeal are concerned. The masterly creation of artistic expression, however, reached its zenith in the carving of *apsarās* at the temple of Angkor Wat. Application of the term "institution" to *apsarās* at Angkor Wat will not be inappropriate if one takes into account the number occupying every part of the massive temple. A visitor is simply spellbound by the variety of headdresses, facial expressions and the flowing drapery covering only a part of the body. The realization in sculpture of exquisite feminine beauty not only enchants the mind, but also speaks of the penetrating comprehension of the artists, so much so that they could generate life in stone. The *apsarās* in their representation here appear full of youth and life in their fascinating expressions.

Art in every part of the world developed under the patronage of kings and Cambodia was no exception. Besides dealing with various religious and secular subjects, the artists also included life in the courts, and the depiction of many *apsarās*, particularly at Angkor Wat, brings out a very important part of the life of the king. A life-size representation of the scene of the Churning of the Ocean in which Viṣṇu played the leading role, also finds majestic expression in the South-Eastern corner of the third enclosure. Free carving of *apsarās* in large number should be viewed primarily against this background because they spring from the Ocean at the time of the Churning, and the king Sūryavarman II considered himself, in the capacity of *devarāja*, to be *de facto* Viṣṇu.

Found in almost every part of the temple of Angkor Wat, the *apsarās* seem to vie with each other, in dress, decoration and seductive position, for the attention of the divine king. One could easily write a dissertation on the *apsarās* at Angkor Wat, taking into consideration the large number of headdresses, facial expressions and the position in which the *apsarās* stand. Some examples of facial features, for instance, reveal the existence of several races, which might represent women captured in war. The graceful forms of the *apsarās* have been chiselled out both singly (Pl. 7.3) and in groups of two to six.

Their headdresses are of various kinds, for example fan-shaped or cap-and crown-like, revealing Mongolian and Chinese features. The headdresses are almost invariably crowned above with long-stemmed flowers, emerging prominently above the head like plumes, with multiple circular decorated jewels affixed.

Though the breasts differ in proportions, they are all round and life-like, with the nipples sometimes only suggested. In some examples, the *apsarās* have been carved with the hand touching the breast. The hips are broad and heavy, the waist slender and supple. The suppleness depicted in the curvature of the body is full of amorous appeal.

Veils are foreign to *apsarās*, though not completely unknown. Of the diaphanous drapery (Pl. 7.4) only the flowing part on either side of the feet can be observed in various styles. The folds of the flowing lower garment are in many cases held on the arm near the elbow, with part of it falling on the other side.

Following a course entirely different from India, heavy ornaments (Pl. 7.5) were not generally used by *apsarās* as an aid to beauty. Necklaces and waistbands of several strands adorned with triangular pendants, and two heavy anklets were almost universally worn. Circular lockets dangling against the bosom, heavy suspended earrings of various designs and decorated waistbands, besides many kinds of headdresses, are some of the simple ornaments that used to adorn the body. The hair is arranged in various ways, sometimes parted on two sides, and the forehead is often ornamented with a broad diamond-shaped auspicious mark.

The hands of the *apsarās* depicted alone are in different positions: generally bent at right angles to touch the stomach (Pl. 7.6), they are often curved and resting on the hip, or one of the hands may be raised to touch the headdress. *Apsarās* have also been systematically portrayed with flowers held in a raised hand. Mirrors of different shapes are occasionally held in the hand, and play-objects in a raised hand are also often seen. Occasionally both the hands are folded at right angles to meet near the navel, which has been shown prominently. In groups, the hand of one may be resting on the shoulder of another as if about to embrace, and sometimes the hand of one is intertwined with the other. The feet are always depicted turned sideways.

The eyes of the *apsarās* are expressive of an invitation to enjoyment and revelry, and with the same end in view, the slim body and head are bent in a voluptuous manner. Flowers were a source of great delight to the women of Cambodia and consequently many *apsarās* have been carved below thick floral decoration; similarly the headdress may also be covered with every kind of flower.

*Apsarās* were carved before being fixed in position in the temple. Inspiration for erecting massive monuments was no doubt generated by the Indian influence, but in accordance with local conventions and traditions they developed a style of their own. Unlike in India, the *apsarās* in the monuments of Cambodia are not in very high relief. In spite of the fact that there is free expression of feminine beauty, coital scenes in multiple poses do not find any place on the monuments, irrespective of the fact that they are so common in India. Depiction of couples appears to have been a taboo in Cambodia. Similarly there is a fundamental departure from the Indian tradition in the expression of full nudity, for there are no such examples to be seen in Cambodia.

## NOTES AND REFERENCES

1. Malcolm MacDonald, *Angkor*, London, Jonathan Cape, 1958, p. 77
2. *Ibid.*, p. 79.
3. Peter T. White, "The Temples of Angkor: Ancient Glory in Stone", edited and photography by Wilbur E. Garrett, *National Geographic*, 161 (5), May 1982, p. 548.
4. Vetham Mani, *Puranic Encyclopaedia*, Delhi, 1979, p. 46.
5. A. Cunningham, *The Stūpa of Bharhut*, Varanasi, 1962, p. 27.
6. T.A. Gopinath Rao, *Elements of Hindu Iconography*, II, Delhi, 1968, p. 561.
7. Goldstücker, *Sanskrit Dictionary*, pp. 222-23.

# 8

# Lao Tai Muang and Art Manifestation

A.K. Das

Laos is a landlocked country surrounded by Thailand, Cambodia, Vietnam and Burma (now Myanmar). The Mekong River which flows from the north to south forms the narrow valley bordering Thailand. The remaining part of the country is a hilly terrain rising above the Mekong River. The very ecology dictates subsistence level of economy based on the paddy cultivation. The rice growing plain here is contiguous with Thailand and Myanmar which creates an age-old cultural affinity in this region.

Fifty per cent of the Laotian population, inhabiting in the river valley, are the ethnic Tai. Those who live in the hills are tribals and others namely Khmu, Akha, Hmongs, etc. The Lao Tai mythology takes their origin to North Vietnam (Dien Bien Phu). It is believed that they were born out of a gourd opened by one Khon Borom. The Khon Borom's seven sons, according to legend, moved in seven directions and established seven kingdoms. The migration history of the Tais from China and their spread over South-East Asia is well known. The formation of the Tai Muang, kingdom in Thailand in around 12th century AD and existence of the Tai cultural pool in Vietnam, Laos and Thailand are recorded history.[1]

Laotians are culturally more closer to the people of Thailand than any other people of the neighbouring countries because of the presence of Tai Muangs. According to some scholars, the formation of Muang state took place as a result of coming together several clans under one chieftain (Chao Muang). In fact, Muangs retain their identity through certain social and material tradition till today irrespective of their time, space and migration history.[2]

At least three important factors govern the cultural relationship of the Tai, no matter whether they live in Laos, Myanmar, Thailand, Cambodia, Vietnam and even in the North-Eastern part of India. The factors are paddy cultivation, Buddhism and Tai Muangs. The cultural homogeneity in South-East Asia is governed by the identical ecology, the resultant material way of life and corresponding art manifestations—all woven together by the above three factors.

The Mekong River valley on the both sides covers Myanmar, Thailand and Laos—topographically a region of wet-rice cultivation except for the hills where slash and burn cultivation is the norm. The annual agricultural cycle in this region is a common paradigm. This has its manifestations in the belief and practices which have given rise to similar rites, rituals, fairs and festivals, no matter whether Buddhist or "traditional religions practices". These indigenous practices have greatly contributed to the traditional performing arts and various other non-performing symbolic visual art forms.

The Laotians' main religion is Hīnayāna form of Buddhism which like Thailand and Myanmar came here in 5th or 6th century AD. There is, however, an undercurrent of the Hindu philosophy as evident from the existing performing arts such as mask dances or shadow puppets based on the Rāmāyaṇa story in same manner as that of Thailand or Cambodia. From 14th century onwards, we find certain art forms in dramatic representation such as mask dances, puppet performances and classical form of dance. There are multiple representations in the performing art derived from the *Jātaka* tales. There is invariably the influence of Khmer and Thai styles presentation in their forms of art.[3] Among the mask dances, *Lagor* and *Khon* dance drama could be associated with the court performances of Luang Prabang and neighbouring areas. There is no doubt that the *Lagor*, a female performance, and the *Khon*, a male performance are extension of *Thai Lakhan* and *Khon* dance drama contextually as well as stylistically. Besides, the indigenous masked performance *Phou noy* is a part of magico-religious beliefs and practices and the main image represented here may be considered as a different form of Indian Kinnari, a mythical anthropomorphic creature (half-woman and half-bird). This is performed as a part of magico-religious ritual for invoking rain. Besides, as a new year festivities masked performance of *Phou Genu* is performed to commemorate the sacrifice of *Phou Tae Genu* and *Me Genam*, the ancestors of Lao people who brought Choread the Liana from earth and ended the engulfing darkness. Their dances have now become part of Buddhist rituals because of the very content of dance. The wooden masks used in the dance reveal typical South-East Asian style of awe-inspiring and monumentality having long strands of jute fibre hanging from the mask to the face of the dancer.[4]

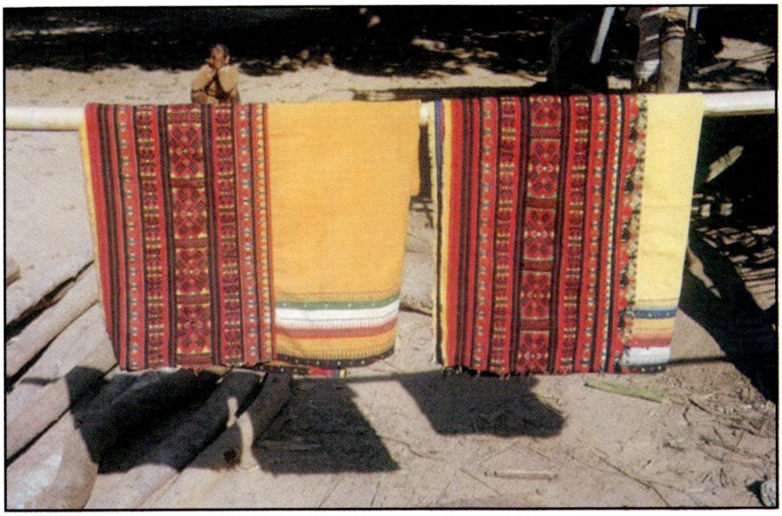

Pl. 8.1. Tribal textile design, Assam.

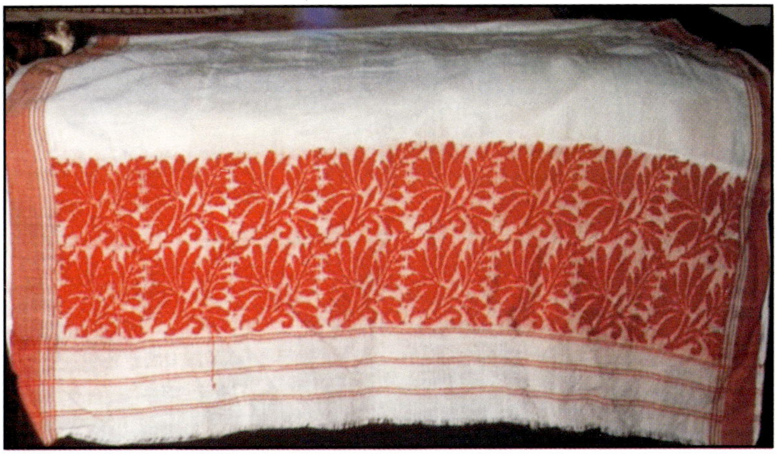

Pl. 8.3. Gamucha (towel), Assam.

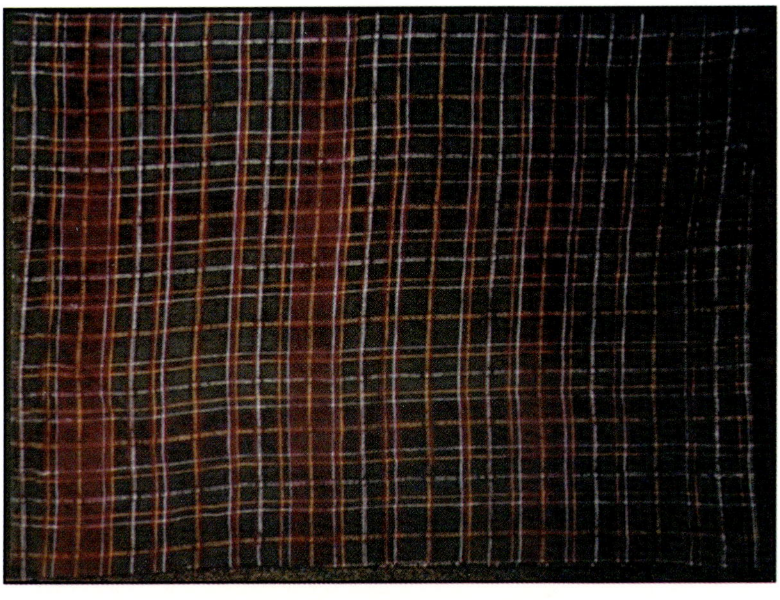

Pl. 8.6. Lower garment of males, Khamti, Arunachal Pradesh.

Pl. 8.4. Sash, Khamti, Arunachal Pradesh.

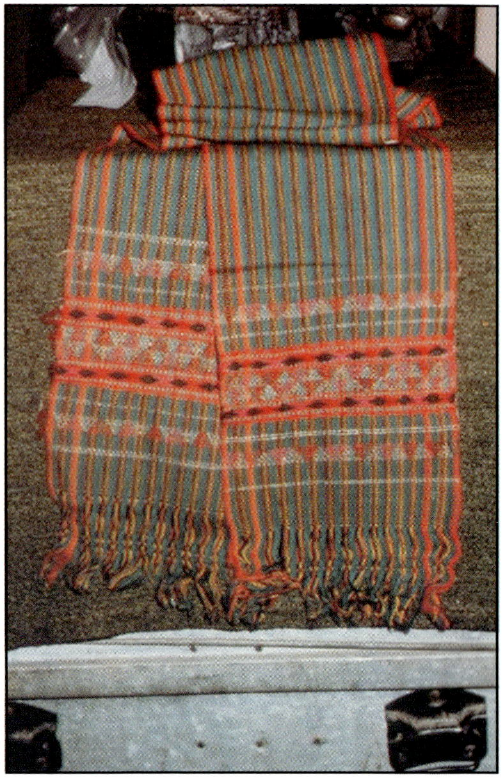

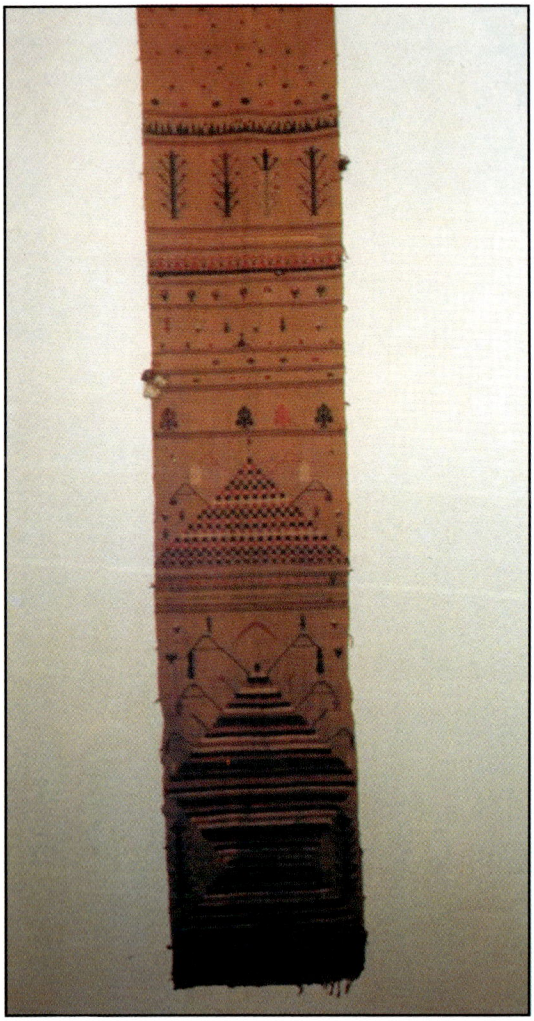

Pl. 8.2. Tankhawn, a religious banner.

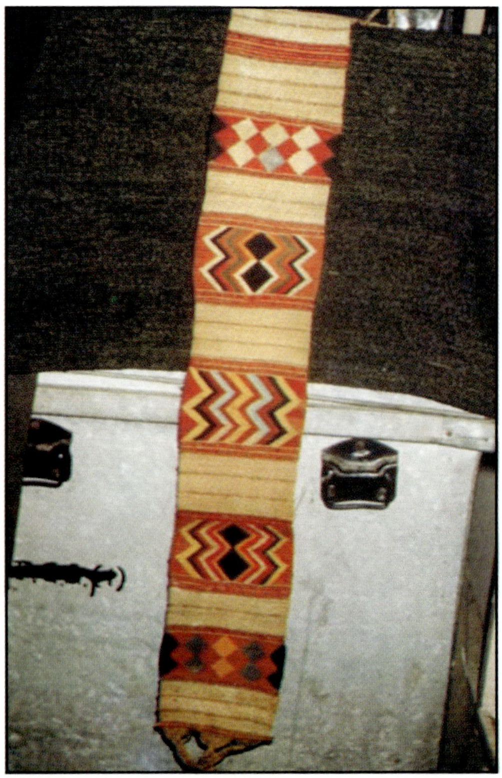

Pl. 8.5. Sash, Naga, Nagaland.

The puppets, both shadow and rod type, are performed at the time of Rocket Festival (*boun bang fay*) marking the *nirvaṇa* (salvation) of Buddha. In spite of its distinct characteristic, the Lao shadow puppet is an extension of the Khmer and Thai models; in both the cases stories from the Rāmāyaṇa are invariably of great inspiration along with warrior legends, religious myths, folk-tales, etc. Besides the Rocket Festival, puppet shows were also performed after the mortuary rites along with dance and other entertainments.

Understanding of the significance of certain art forms, such as textile motifs, manner and occasion of the use of certain traditional apparels and items of dress are very important to comprehend the cohesiveness of the Tai Muang in this region. The apparels such as woman's headdress, skirts, shoulder cloth, waistband and to some extent the upper garment (blouse and jacket) are the distinctive symbol of identity and image of the wearer. According to Naenna, the female costume was once a method of expressing solidarity and allegiance in addition to the identification of the ethnic group, village, social and economic status etc.[5] This is because of the accepted norm evolved sometime in 11th or 12th century at the time of the formation of larger and powerful Muang State by bringing together different smaller kindred groups. After the formation of Muang State, the social and political set-up also underwent changes and influenced women's costumes and textile patterns.

At present, the regional and ethnic varieties of Laotian textile could be seen in different provinces such as Luang Prabang, Hua Phan, Xiang Khowang, Vientiene, etc. Even certain urban centres in different provinces could be connected with distinct textile patterns such as Sam Nena, Luang Prabang, Muang Thaeng (Vietnam), etc.

In Sam Nena of Hua Phan province, there are different groups of Tais collectively known as Tai Nena which could be easily identified from their textiles. One of the subgroups, here the Tai Daneng, produces textile with intricate patterns. Some of the textiles are woven for special occasions like funeral ceremony. The *sin mi* (skirt) with alternating bands of weft *ikat* and supplementary weft are worn by the kinsman of the deceased himself. Along with the *sin mi*, a waistband (*hoa buan*) is given to the dead for safe passage to the other world (garden of golden mango). Besides, in certain magico-religious rites, indigo shawls having special patterns are used by the shamans. The motifs in these textiles pieces are mostly geometric, zoomorphic as well as anthropomorphic representing spirit. The shamans also used a narrower sash like headband with similar patterns. Besides these animist designs and patterns, since 1st millennium AD, Buddhist symbols were incorporated in Tai Dang textiles such as temples, flags, lion and *nāga* or *nak*. The *nak* figure is considered to be ancient than the Indian *nāga* and most probably a river dragon associated with fertility cult. In course of time, the *nak* became more realistic and more elaborate with supplementary *ikat* technique.[6]

The *Tai Dams,* another group of *Tai Naea* textiles, are identical with that of the Tai Dang having less complex bands of supplementary wefts. In Xiang Khoang province, the Tai Pher, an ethnic group, adhering to traditional beliefs and practices weave woman's skirt having zoomorphic, geometric and anthropomorphic patterns brought out by supplementary warp on evenly distributed strips throughout, specially for red sash or shoulder cloth. The Tai Pher of southern Laos (Savanakhet province) weave similar textiles.

The Tai Lue, who are scattered in different provinces after their migration from South China,[7] could be categorically distinguished with tapestry weaving in Laos. The most important characteristic of Tai Lue skirt is the combination of different weaving techniques dominated by tapestry, supplementary weft and weft *ikat*. The arrangement of the decorative element is such that the strips are seen in a horizontal plane and this gives distinction to the *Tai Lue* textiles wherever it is noticed. The weaving motifs are confined to geometric in most cases and anthropomorphic in some cases. *Tai Lue* textiles in Laos are mostly cotton and rarely silk. A shoulder cloth *pha chet* with red and black supplementary pattern is specially woven by women folk for their beloved.

The royal family and the members of the court in Luang Prabang and Vientiane provinces in Laos used distinct type of textiles since 15th century. These textiles resemble the *ikat* designs of the Indian *patola*. The technique used here is weft *ikat* having red as base colour. Besides, there are Indian brocades specially in the repertoire of royal costumes along with Chinese satin cloth embroidered with gold and silver thread by local craftsman. They are quite exquisite.

The hill people, mostly tribals, have distinctive clothes, specially a variety of headdresses. The *akha* or Hmong women's costume are very attractive and colourful, decorated with embroidery and applique work. Sometimes *batik* technique is also applied. Embroidered patterns are geometric. Occasionally stylised zoomorphic motifs in very distinct form are also noticed. These ethnic groups weave and dye their clothes with their traditional technique. The colour composition in each case is distinct which gives them their identity whether headdress or body apparels.

It has already been stated that the Tai Muang, wherever they spread, maintained their identity in spite of their assimilation with local population. This, we have seen in Vietnam, Myanmar and Cambodia. In North-East India especially Assam and Arunachal Pradesh, we have Tai population, migrated sometime in 13th century AD, completely assimilated with local population taking their language and religion and other customs. I am referring here the Ahom population of Assam, who ruled for 600 years. The textile designs (Pl. 8.1) and patterns, dresses and costumes, silk rearing and spinning were brought by these people from South-East Asia. Tai Assamese women's skirt (*mekhalā*) with *butadiya* pattern, shoulder cloth (*rehā*) with *kesh basa* technique and *gamuchā* (Pl. 8.3) (towel) with typical *fulam* pattern of red weft supplementary technique are nothing but the tradition of the Tais that even spread to the tribal areas. The latter migration of Tai people from Shan province which entered Assam through Patkoi range settled in upper Brahmaputra valley in and around Dibrugarh. They are presently regarded as tribal population because of their distinct way of living. They are Tai-Fake or Fakia, Aitonia, Duwania, Khamiyang, Khamti and Singpho. These people, to some extent, retained their language, religion, their costumes and textile patterns.

Although the woman's dresses, sober in colour and composition, have undergone some changes but the stiched skirt (*mekhelā*) and the shoulder cloth (*chādar*) are still continued and used in a similar fashion. The textile motifs, specially the floral, zoomorphic, anthropomorphic and geometric supplementary weft technique, are continued in a more simple manner. The multiple colour composition of the Tai Dang and other Laotian textile patterns replaced by single colour, generally in red or white background. The *nak* pattern has been greatly transformed to become a sort of zig-zag motif with stylisation. The diamond pattern, as found in the head-scarf of shaman in Laos, which is considered by some scholars as Mahāyāna symbol of third eye[8] is woven individually and collectively in the Assamese textiles such as *chādar*, *rehā* and *mekhelā*. These patterns have been copied by some tribes such as Apatani, Mishmi, Adi representing different symbols in North-East.

The contemporary textiles of the Khamtis (Pl. 8.6) and Singphos of Arunachal Pradesh show retention of the Tai motifs specially in their skirts and shoulder cloth of womenfolk, cotton bags, religious banners, etc. The Khamti textile bags and the religious banners show elaborate Tai textile designs brought out by the supplementary weft techniques. One of the Singpho religious banners is a replica of Tung Yai (webbed flags), a banner made by the Tai Phuan people for use in important festivals. These flags were originally protective in nature. The Khamti and Singhpo banners (*tankhawn*) (Pl. 8.2) are made in bamboo frame wrapped by coloured threads in the same manner as Tung Yai. There is innovation of the original square-shaped webbed flags. Here there are *tankhawn* having circular motifs in bamboo frame wrapped with threads in different colours giving them the shape of cobweb.

If we take the functional aspect of the dress, costumes, textile designs and motifs, we notice a similar situation in North-East India as that of Laos. The image and identify of a person within the group or outside the group could be established by the following criteria:

1. Manner of wearing
2. Use in particular part of the body
3. Colour composition
4. Design and motifs
5. Technique of weaving
6. Nature of the yarn

In the first instance, use of a particular cloth such as women's skirt could be instantly related to a particular tribe or ethnic group. As for example, the fourteen Nāga groups could be identified from their textile (Pl. 8.5) pattern. In Arunachal Pradesh, there are 12 subgroups of the Adis. These groups could be identified from their respective textiles (Pl. 8.4). The status of a person such as a noted chieftain, a Konyak headhunter, an Apatani priest, an Angami wealthy man, a married Assamese woman an unmarried Adi girl is subjected to typical textiles. The Assamese *bihuwan* is a representative of the *phachet—a* shoulder cloth woven as love gift for a man in Laos.

Probably, symbolic identification of one's own group solidarity is a cultural pre-requisite in South-East Asia, which took shape in 12th-13th centuries due to the inter-ethnic interface of transmigration and their permeation in different regions and gradual assimilation.

## NOTES AND REFERENCES

1. W.C. Dodd, *Tai Race: Elder Brother of the Chinese,* Cedar Rapids, lowa, 1923.
2. Eric Seidenfaden, *The Tai peoples,* Bangkok, 1958.

3. Frank M. Lebar (ed.), *Laos: Its People, Its Society and Its culture*, New Havean, 1960.
4. J.O. Miettinien, *Classical Dance and Theatre in South-East Asia*, Singapore, 1992.
5. Patricia Naenna, *Costume and Culture: Vanishing Textiles of Some of the Tai Groups in Laos P. D.R.*, Chiang Mai, 1990, p. 1.
6. *Ibid.*, p. 3.
7. Conway Susan, *Thai Textiles*, 1992, p. 106.
8. Patricia Naenna, *op. cit.*, p. 3.

# 9

# Buddhist Art of Laos

Bachchan Kumar

The Buddhist art of Laos has been a matter of discussion among the scholars. A limited number of Laotian artefacts of ancient period have been discovered. Therefore, it is very difficult to trace out the origin of the different motifs of this art style. The present paper examines Buddhist art and architecture of Laos and links it with the art styles of the neighbouring countries with particular reference to Indian art styles.

A large number of scholars notably Waddell, Grunwedel, Foucher, Burgess, Getty, Coomaraswamy, Bhattasali, Bhattacharyya, R.D. Banerjee and many others have written useful and authoritative works and collected together a considerable amount of information on Buddhist art of India. Getty and Deniker's *Gods of Northern Buddhism* deals with Tibetan, Chinese and Japanese gods. A. Foucher, for the first time, drew attention of the scholars to Buddhist art by publishing his work *Etudes sur I'Iconographie Bouddhique de I'Inde* in two parts as early as 1900 and 1905. He studied the miniatures on the Buddhist manuscript, the *Prajñāpāramitā*, and then made a systematic attempt to identify the sculptures. For the purpose of recognising images he hunted out a number of *sādhanās* from the manuscripts of *Sādhanamālā*, and was surprised to find that the images, tallied most remarkably with the description given in the unpublished texts of tantric manuscripts. Foucher's second volume embodies a critical, although partial study of the *Sādhanamālā* and it was this book that first emphasised the necessity of referring to a *sādhanā* in a order to make or justify any single identification of a Buddhist image.

The Laotian Buddhist art has not been analysed in detail. Henri Mouhot did an exploratory work which came to light through his diary. The diary was abridged and edited by Christopher Pym.[1] Perala Ratnam's work entitled *Laos and Its Culture* has dealt with the

Rāmāyaṇa in relation to other aspects of Laotian culture.[2] Henri Parmentier's work *l'art du Laos* is an authoritative work which describes Laotian art in general. Sachchidanand Sahai has done commendable work and published books namely Rāmāyaṇa *in Laos: A Study in Gvāy Dvoraḥbī, Phra Lăk Phra Lām, Kṛṣṇa Saga in Laos,* etc. These works are the translation of Laotian manuscripts based on the Rāmāyaṇa and the Mahābhārata. During early times, Laotians adapted Indian literary works to suit their customs, manners and cultural traditions. The Rāmāyaṇa and the Mahābhārata stories were transformed and assimilated in Buddhist tradition. The transformation was so complete and the assimilation so perfect that these literary traditions have become part of their national life and product of their creative genius. Also a unique art style evolved based on Indian art styles. Thus, Coedés has very rightly described Laos as an "out-post" of Indian civilisation.[3]

In the earlier times, Laos was known as Muong Xieng Thong or Laem Thong. Its Sanskrit name was *Souvaṇṇa Phoūm Pathet (Suvarṇabhūmi Pradesh)*. Suvarṇabhūmi Pradesh was a large peninsula situated between the Indian Ocean and the China Sea. Indian traders took regular voyages to these areas. It is very difficult to say why this part of land was named *Suvarṇabhūmi*. R.C. Majumdar and other scholars believe that this land was prosperous for trade and commercial purposes and had the potential for more prosperity, hence it was called *Suvarṇabhūmi*.

The Buddhist texts *Dīpavaṃsa* and *Mahāvaṃsa* give us a glimpse of the over sea journeys undertaken by the Indians. The *Jātaka* stories also testify the fact. The *Samuddavāṇija Jātaka*[4] tells the story of the migration of the family of a carpenter who proceeded along the Gaṅgā for an island home in the overseas. The *Milindapañho*[5] also mentions the regular voyages to various places including *Suvarṇabhūmi*.

> Yathā mahārāja sadhano nāviko paṭṭane suṭṭhu katasuṅko mahāsamuddaṃ pavisitvā Vangaṃ Takkolam Cīnam Sovīram Suraṭṭham Alasandaṃ Kolapaṭṭanaṃ Suvaṇṇabhūmiṃ gacchati aññam pi yaṃ kiñci nāvāsañcaraṇaṃ...

Since remote past, Indians have close contacts with the people of Laos. Indian traders and religious missionaries went through sea and land routes and settled there. Some of them married the local people and introduced their rich cultural heritage to suit the indigenous population. A large part of the population of Laos lives along the Mekong River valley and its tributaries. The word 'Mekong' is the composition of Me=Mā (Mother) and Kong=Gaṅgā. Thus the river

Mekong is the dialectical variation of *Mā Gaṅgā*.[6] It is an obvious evidence of imbibing Indian culture by the Lao people.

## ORIGIN OF THE LAO

The name of the kingdom of Laos is derived from the Lao people, a branch of the Tai ethnic group. For several centuries after the Han period there is no information on the Tai people. During 1st century AD, the Tais were living in Tonkin and settling in the upper valleys. Their increase in population compelled them to move through river valleys to the lower regions of what is now southern Kwangsi province which was under the Chinese command. During the 8th century AD, according to historians, they rebelled twice against the Chinese overlord. Indeed, there are signs that Tai people during the 8th century moved as far north as the Si-Kiang basin, and at the end of that century they intruded into Ho-nan province.[7] Later, they settled there and established the kingdom of Nanchao and made its capital in Yunnan. A relatively well-organised state, Nanchao existed until 1253, when it was destroyed by the Mongols under Kublai Khan.

Chinese expansion, even before the destruction of Nanchao, had brought pressure on these Tai peoples, who gradually migrated farther south. Some Tais, including the present-day Laos, followed the Mekong River into the rugged, sparsely populated northern hinterland of the Khmer empire, which was centred in the modern Cambodia. The inhabitants of this region consisted of two distinct groups. One group was dark skinned, believed by some to have been in the area since early times. The second group was Malayo-Polynesian, who had migrated there sometime between 500 BC and AD 500. There were also some Cham, Mon and Khmer peoples, who may have been of Malayo-Polynesian origin.[8]

Early Lao migration was peaceful—not an invasion—and did not involve large movement of population. Terwiel opines that the Tais spread over mainland South-East Asia as a result of a rapid series of events.[9] The first references to the appearance of the Tais in South-East Asia have been found in Cham inscriptions and the record of Pagan.[10] Also, there exist many indigenous written sources dealing with ancient migration routes as well as with mythological genealogies. One Tai written source claims to go back as far as the 7th century AD.[11] But the peaceful migration of the Tais must have picked up speed by the 11th century AD.

At the beginning of their settlement, the Laos accepted Khmer domination of the tribal organisation and later appeared to have been under the suzerainty of a Tai state to the west in what is now Thailand. Gradually their number increased, they occupied the valley of the Mekong and its tributaries for their wet-rice cultivation displacing earlier inhabitants who then moved to higher altitudes. The collapse of Nanchao state in 13th century accelerated the southward migration of the Tais who reached the areas of North Vietnam, Thailand, Burma (now Myanmar), modern Assam (in North-Eastern part of India) and Hainan island.

## FOUNDATION OF THE LAOTIAN KINGDOM

The early history of Laos is obscure. According to the legends, the earliest known historical king of Central Cambodia, who ruled over Laos as well, is Śrutavarman. He laid foundation of a royal house. Except his son Śreshṭhavarman, the name of other rulers is not known. No doubt, at the beginning of the Christian era, the lower Mekong part of Laos was under the control of the kingdom of Funan (as called by the Chinese) with its capital Vidhayapura and the southern Laos, called Champassak, under the control of the mighty kingdom Champa. Both the kingdoms, Funan and Champa, were founded by Indian settlers. They had Indian conception of royalty, practised Hinduism and used Sanskrit language. Sometime in the second half of the 5th century, however, a vassal of Funan named Śreshṭhavarman was victorious over the Chams of Champassak and founded a city at the foot of a hillside sanctuary, Wat Phu, which had long been the site of a *liṅga* cult closely associated with the Indianised monarchies of ancient Indo-China.[12] The city was named Śhresṭhapūra.

The Khmer's epigraphical records mention that Laos was under the Khmer control till the end of the 12th century. Subsequently, the Thais held sway over certain Laotian territory. By the end of the 13th century, they were in control of the two principal cities Luang Prabang and Vientiane. Then followed political confusion; different royal houses asserted their supremacy. After the downfall of the Thai kingdom, Sukhothai, around AD 1345, a new Thai dynasty was founded in Ayuthia in AD 1349. The weakening of the kingdom of Sukhothai and its submission to the kingdom of Ayuthia favoured the foundation of the Laotian State.

According to Laotian source, Fa Ngum, exiled Lao chief, was brought up at the court of Angkor. The young prince was raised there by a Buddhist preceptor and when he had reached the age of sixteen, the Khmer king gave him one of his own daughters in marriage.

Between AD 1340 and 1350, with the help of Khmer, Fa Ngum took command of an army to reconquer the lost territory of his father in the upper Mekong area. He captured the plateau of Xieng Khouang, Hauaphanh, Sip Song Phanna and Luang Prabang and founded an independent Laotian kingdom. He made his capital at Luang Prabang (Lan Xang; the land of million elephants). In order to expand his territorial boundary, Fa Ngum, later, made a successful expedition against Chieng Mai in the upper Menam Valley and Vientiane. At that time, the Laotian territory was extended up to Champa along the Annamite chain in the east; on the west it was bordered by three Thai kingdoms along the Menam River.[13] It is said that Fa Ngum received tributes from one of the three Thai kingdoms as well as a princess for marriage of his son.

After Fa Ngum, his son, Phya Sam Sene Thai (lord of 300,000 Tais) succeeded to the throne of Lan Xang. The king was married to a Thai princess. No doubt, his territory had large Thai population (around 300,000), thus he was named Phya Sam Sene Thai. The Lan Xang kingdom prospered till 17th century AD which was called the golden age of Laotians. Later, Burmese invasion weakened the empire.

## RISE OF BUDDHISM

Under the Khmer rulers, Buddhism was introduced in Laos and both Mahāyāna and Theravada Buddhism prospered. The early inhabitants of Laos practised spirit (*phi*) worship. The invocation and propitiation of spirits are still in vogue in nearly every village and remained a concern for a large segment of population, especially among the hill tribes. Laotians believe that various types of *phi* are present throughout the universe. They hold great power over the destinies of men. This *phi* concept merged in Buddhism in such a way that it became an integral part of Buddhism. Belief in the *phi* appears not only among the laity but also at the highest levels of the organised Buddhist clergy. Nearly all Lao Buddhists bear a strong element of *phi* worship. A monk may be called into a household in which one of the members is sick in order to participate in the ceremonies and playing music designed to exorcise the malevolent *phi* from the body of the victim. Many monks are thought to have a special knowledge of the *phi.*

The mighty Sukhothai ruler, king Rāma Khamhaeng, in the later part of the 13th century, introduced Theravada Buddhism of the Sinhalese origin.[14] This new religion ideally suited the people but co-existed with the *phi* worship. This form of Buddhism counsels the believers to hold a profound reverence of the Buddha, his teaching (*dhamma*), and the order he founded (*sangha*).

When Fa Ngum took over the charge of the mightly Lao kingdom, the Sinhalese origin Theravada Buddhism was prospering there. He patronised this form of Buddhism and took interest in its propagation.[15] King Fa Ngum sent a mission to Khmer empire to invite a group of monks and artists. This mission brought to Laos a high ranked Khmer monk and artists including the Phra Bang—the golden image of Buddha. This image later became the palladium of the Lao kingdom. Fa Ngum's son and successor Phya Sam Sene Thai also patronised Buddhism.

King Setthathirah, ruler of Lan Xang from 1547 to 1571, made his capital, Vientiane, a holy centre of Theravada Buddhism. During the reign of Souligna Vongsa, which ended in 1694, the official schools for the teaching of Buddhist doctrines were established for the first time in Laos.

## BUDDHIST ART OF LAOS

The real time of the beginning of Buddhist art in Laos is little known. Relatively isolated by the mountainous lands, the Laotians did not develop their own style until, a much later time. As is well known, the construction of religious edifices has been the focal point of artistic endeavour in Laos. Most of the ancient religious buildings, stylistically connected with the Khmer stone architecture, were built of perishable materials and have been destroyed by fire, weather, or wars over several years. Nevertheless, a few remains of the monasteries and *stūpas* of Lan Xang period are still available. They are the variant of the styles of early Thai schools of art. After conquering Ayuthia, the Burmese introduced their own style of art, which can still be discerned subsequently in the roofs of certain edifices and other artefacts. Laotian art objects are to a great extent influenced by the Khmer, Thai and of later period by the Burmese but the principles are based on Indian art styles.

## SCULPTURE

A number of Buddhist sculptures have been found in different parts of Laos. Their date varies from 7th century AD to the late 18th century AD. The images are beautifully carved showing the technical skills and the aesthetic sense of the artists. The sculptors built their sculptures following the principles of Indian iconography. From the iconographic details it appears that the Laotian sculptors were well aware of every element of Buddhist iconography. The images of Buddha display prominently the symbols characterising a great person, i.e. *mahāpuruṣa lakṣanaṁ.*

The early sculptures of the 7th century, found near Vientiane, are a testimony of the influence of largely Mon-Khmer art of Dvārāvati, a style of art which flourished in the central part of Thailand and was based on Gupta and post-Gupta art styles of India.[16] This art style appeared around 7th century AD and continued till the 11th century AD. According to Diskul,[17] this style of art flourished until it was conquered by the Thais in the late 13th century AD.

During the 11th to the 13th century AD, Mahāyāna Buddhism was very popular in major parts of Laos. This religious sect was not only prevalent among the ruling classes but also practised by the common and ethnic population of the country. The effigy of Jayavarman VII (reigning AD 1181-1220), transformed into the image of the Buddha, sitting in Samādhī posture (near That Luang, Vientiane) and the stele of the hospitals (AD 1186; Vientiane) bear witness to the presence of Mahāyāna Buddhism in the area. The present ethnic textiles also indicate the wide prevalence of Mahāyāna Buddhism in Laos during ancient times.

The transformation of the image of Jayavarman VII into the Buddha testifies to the fact that the Devarāj cult was prevalent in Laos. It was a tantric cult started by the Khmer ruler Jayavarman II (who acceded in AD 802) to ensure that the country of the Kambuja would no longer be dependent on Java and that there would be no more than one sovereign ruler [in this kingdom] who would be *cakravartin* (an universal monarch). The ritual connected to this cult was performed by Hiraṇyadāma, a learned Brahman, well versed in magical science, who came from Janapada[18] (India). The Brahman performed the rituals according to the sacred *Vināśikha* text, and other three texts, i.e. the *Nayottara,* the *Sammoha,* and the *Śiraccheda* were recited from beginning to end.[19] After the introduction of this cult, a large part of the state-policies, adopted by the kings, was based on it.

While establishing themselves in the Mekong basin, the Lao people came in touch with the doctrines of Theravada Buddhism (Doctrines of the Elders) as laid down in the Pali canons. Like the Thais and Khmers, the Laotians adopted this form of Buddhism during 13th century but it got official status and became prominent throughout Laos only during the reign of King Fa Ngum. Two statues of the

Pl. 9.2. Buddha in *bhūmisparśa mudrā*, bronze, Chiengsaen style, AD 1450, southern part of Laos.

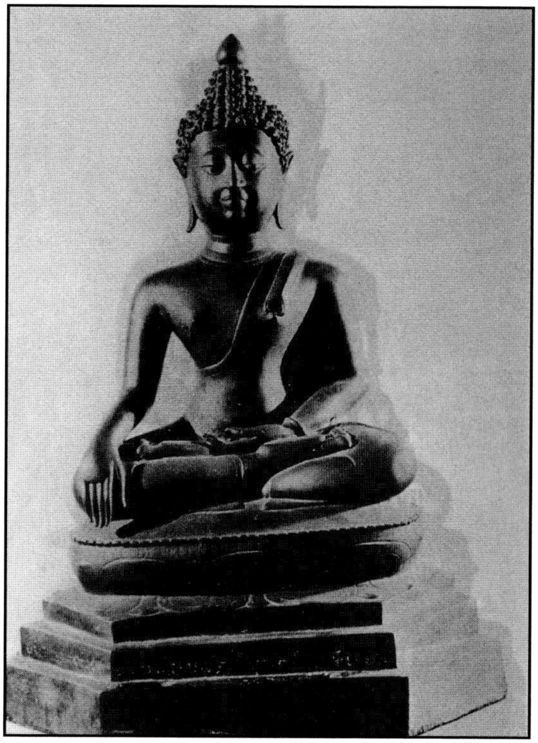

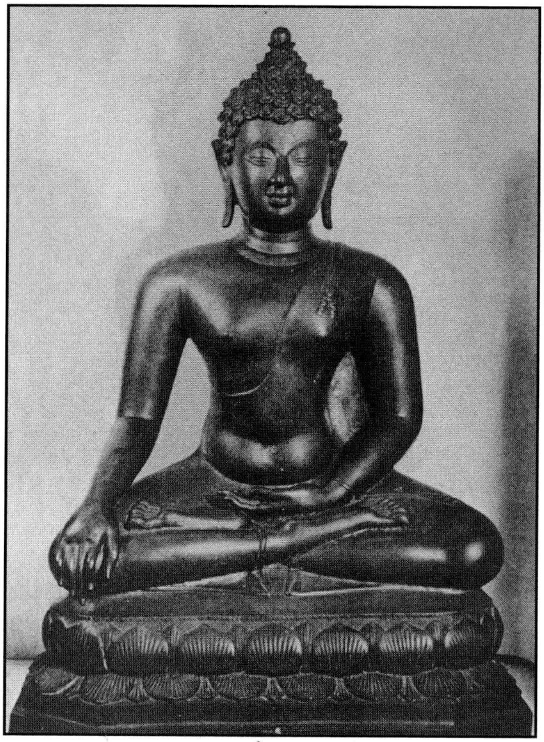

Pl. 9.1. Buddha in *bhūmisparśā mudrā*, bronze, early Chiengsaen style, 11th-13th centuries AD, southern part of Laos.

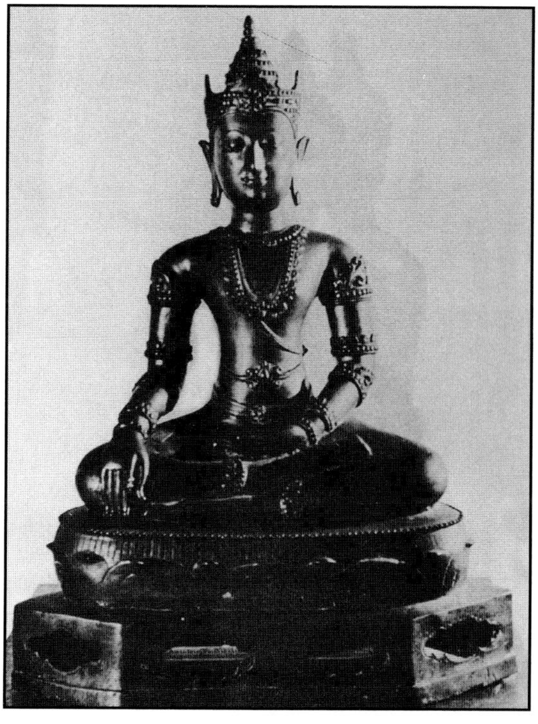

Pl. 9.3. Crowned Buddha in *bhūmisparśa mudrā*, bronze, Chiengmai style, 15th-16th centuries AD, southern part of Laos.

Pl. 9.5. Buddha in *bhūmisparśa mudrā*, bronze, Ayuthia style, 14th century AD, southern part of Laos.

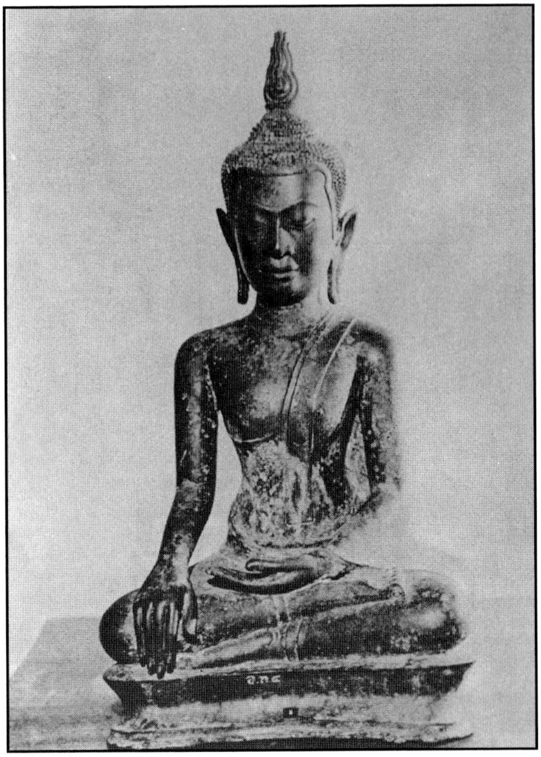

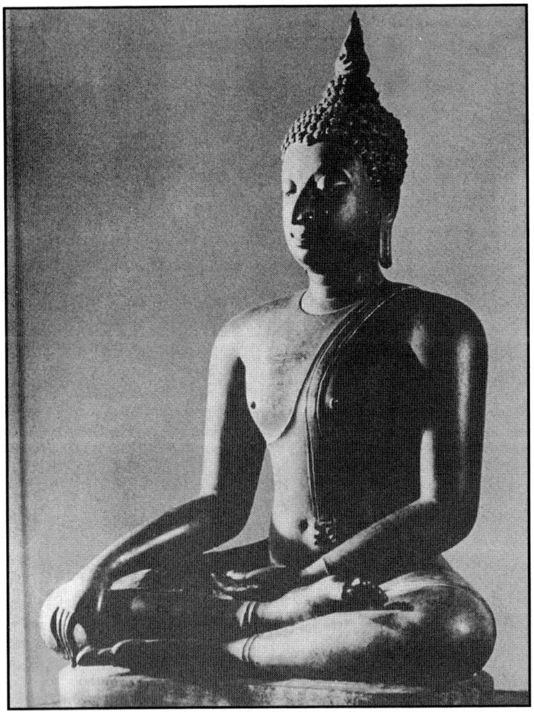

Pl. 9.4. Buddha in *bhūmisparśa mudrā*, bronze, Sukhothai style, 14th century AD, southern part of Laos.

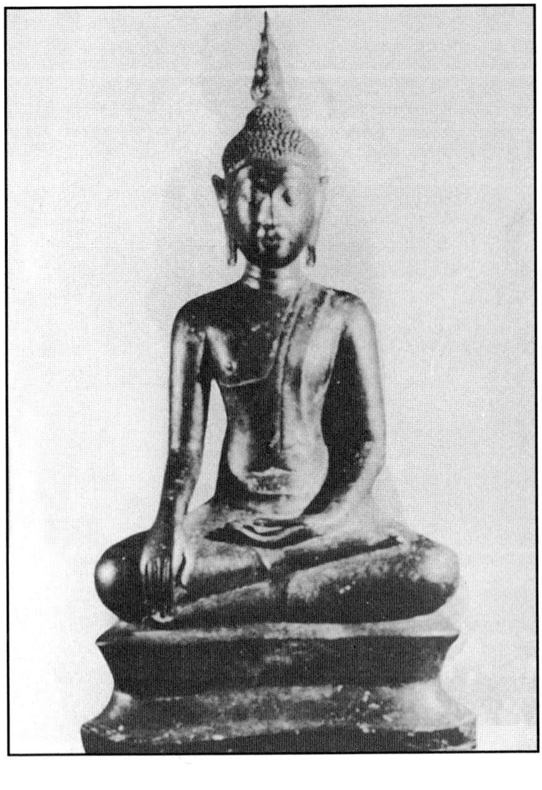

Pl. 9.6. Buddha in *bhūmisparśa mudrā*, bronze, Ayuthia style, 14th-15th centuries AD, southern part of Laos.

Buddha (Luang Prabang; sanctuary of Vat That Luong) were certainly brought by a Khmer mission to the royal court of King Fa Ngum and were erected at a site where a sanctuary was later built.

Few Buddha images of Chiengsaen style (flourished in the northern part of Thailand during 11th to 18th centuries) have been reported from the southern part of Laos. Diskul opines that the images of this style have great resemblance to the Pāla art of India. The images display lotus bud (Pl. 9.1) form *uṣṇīṣa*, a round face with arched eyebrows and a prominent chin, a stout body with a developed chest, the short end of the monastic dress terminating in the notch design on the left shoulder. The images are in *bhūmisparsha mudra* in crossed-leg seated (Pl. 9.2) posture. Jean Boisselier, however, disagrees with the view that this style resembles Pāla art. He opines that the right hand of the early Chiengsaen Buddha is not placed on the middle of the right leg like the Pāla Buddha image but is reposed on the right knee. One may think that these images are very near to the style of Indian Buddha images at Sirpur in Madhya Pradesh and the images of the 8th or 9th century from Virat Cuttack in Orissa.

Some of the Buddha images of Chiengsaen style were carved beautifully and were heavily jewelled (Pl. 9.3). They were probably made at an advanced stage of this style of art. Diskul classifies the Chiengsaen art style in two groups: the early and the late Chiengsaen style. The early Chiengsaen style reveals the features of Burmese art as it came through Pagan in Burma. The late Chiengsaen art is influenced by Śrivijaya art style but it seems to be the Sinhalese of South Indian workmanship. The crowned Buddha image can be cited as an example of late Chiengsaen art style. The image represents the future Buddha, Maitreya or the Buddha himself disguised as an emperor. This seated Buddha image is placed on the lotus pedestal. The Buddha is shown bedecked with necklace, armlets, waistband and anklets. The images of this art style are found in Luang Prabang, Vientiane and Champassak (Bassak). One of the most remarkable characteristics of this art style is that most of the images of Buddha are shown on a highly decorated pedestal.

The Laotian Buddhist sculptures, revealing Sukhothai art style, have also been discovered. The Sukhothai style, regarded as the most original Thai artistic expression, flourished during late 13th century and continued up to early 15th century AD. The bronze images of walking Buddha, with a round face, are regarded as an innovation of Sukhothai artists. The Sukhothai artists were greatly influenced by the Sinhalese art. The flame-like *uṣṇīṣa*, found at the centre of the

Buddha head, is the stylised form of *uṣṇīṣa* of the Sinhalese origin. The Buddha images of Sukhothai style are generally characterised by small hair-curls, an oval face, arched eyebrows, a hooked nose and a smiling expression. The shoulders are large but the waist is small. The hanging flap of the cloth on the left shoulder is quite long down to the navel and terminates in a folded design. The Buddha is usually seated in a folded-leg fashion and is in the attitude of *bhūmisparśa mudrā* (Pl. 9.4). The pedestal of the images is shown plain.

The credit of introducing Sukhothai style of art in Laos goes to a Sukhothai sovereign who sought refuge in the city of Luang Prabang. The Sukhothai art style must have reached Luang Prabang in around late 14th century. During that period, several sacred Buddha images were carved. Even this art style in Laos continued up to 18th century AD. Two Sukhothai styled walking Buddhas of 17th to 18th centuries AD have been discovered in Laos.[20]

Some of the Buddha images of Ayuthia style have also been reported from Laos. The Ayuthia style flourished in the central part of Thailand. This style of art began in the middle of the 14th century AD and lasted upto the 18th century AD. This style of art is an amalgamation of Khmer and Sukhothai art styles. The sculptures of the Ayuthia art style can be divided into two parts: early and later Ayuthia art style. The early Ayuthia art belongs to the second half of the 14th century AD. The face of the images is square with a small band dividing the hair from the forehead. Hair curls exist on the head and at the centre the *uṣṇīṣa* is flame-like (Pl. 9.5) as in Sukhothai sculptures. The eyebrows form more or less a bow. The images bear a gentle smile. The end of the robe on the left shoulder extends down to the navel and terminates in a straight line. The seated posture is in a folded leg fashion (Pl. 9.6). The later period of the Ayuthian sculptures belongs to end of the 14th or beginning of the 15th century AD. The sculptures of this period differ from the early period in refinement and the face structure of the sculptures is oval-shaped.

After the destruction of Ayuthia by the Burmese in AD 1767, a new style of art developed in Laos which was greatly influenced by the Burmese art. The 18th century artefacts of Laos testify to this fact. A bronze Buddha head (Pl. 9.7) found at Vat Phra Kheo, Vientiane of the 18th century, displays the features of the Burmese art style. Moreover, it retains the features of the Sukhothai art. As a result of the amalgamation of the two art styles, the Laotian artists developed a kind of geometrical stylisation of the facial presentation with subtle smile. The nose is pointed and the folds of the neck are clumsy. It appears to be copied from the Siamese model. The hair on the Buddha head is depicted as small conical curls. The globular eyes are surmounted by distinctively incised arched eyebrows.

A beautiful sculpture of the Buddha of the 18th century in *dhyana mudra* (in meditation) seated on a pedestal has been found from north-west part of Laos (Pl. 9.8). The image is characterised by a full face, subtle smile, sharp heavy nose, and globular eyes surmounted by distinctively incised arched eyebrows. The ears are elongated stylised in snail shaped, a characteristic of all the later Laotian Buddha sculptures. The slightly hooked nose seems to continue the line of the forehead. The image, in princely dress, wears an elegant crown on the head. The conspicuous armlets on both the arms adorn the image. At the centre of the head is *uṣṇīṣa* depicted in conical shape which is a characteristic feature of the Burmese images of the Buddha.

A bronze standing Buddha sculpture showing crossed hands touching the waist (Pl. 9.9) has been found at Vat Phra Keo, Vientiane. The image appears to be very naturalistic but exceptional. It reveals the characteristics of late phase of Laotian art. The *uṣṇīṣa* has a flamelike appearance. The Buddha wears clinging robes, beginning with the neck in several folds, and gathered in at the waist by a belt having a round buckle which is like a navel. The rendering of the monastic robe (*uttarāsaṅga)* so that the undergarment (*antravāsaka*) can be seen beneath is intended to express the luminosity of the Buddha's body. The lower part of the robe falls straight but is curved at the end.

## ARCHITECTURE

In Laos, very few ancient religious buildings are found. The ruins of the ancient monuments reveal the fact that the monuments were built only after proper planning of the architects. The Laotian monuments of Khmer period were made of magnificent blocks of stone and derived from the superb Khmer classic styles of Angkor period. The architectural works of the monuments in Bassac and in Angkor area can be cited as an example. With the passage of time, the materials used for their constructions were mainly bricks and stucco. The later phase of architecture was modified by the Thais and Burmese which were confined to the area of southern Laos. The Ayuthian Thai architectural style can be easily traced in Laotian architecture. The style of Chieng Mai is evident in the steep upward sweep of Laotian wat roofs. As in other countries of South-East Asia, Laotian Buddhist monuments still survive in the form of *vihāras, stūpas* and pagodas.

## *VIHĀRA* (MONASTERY)

The *vihāra* or monastery is a residential place of the Buddhist monks which has its own architectural features. The word *vihāra, ārāma,* and *saṅghārāma* are generally used as synonyms. In the beginning, the disciples of the Buddha used to stay in the gardens adjacent to towns and hence their residences were known as *ārāmas.* During early times, there were various *ārāmas* built by the monks in northern India. The famous among them were Jetavanārāma, Veluvanārāma and Kukkutārāma.

The *vihāras* were originally a hutment made of a perishable material (usually of wood and leaves) occupied by a single monk. They were made for passing the *vassa* period of the monks. Soon after the completion of *vassa*, the monks used to dismantle the whole structure and then they left the place. Thus, there are no remains of *vihāras* of the early times in Laos.

Later, the *vihāras* was transformed into partitioned apartments and allotted to a small group of monks. A common storage room was added for the purpose of the storage of articles. In course of time, the *vihāras* were built of durable materials within a compound wall or fenced boundaries and their maintenance was looked after by the donors. This attracted the monks in greater numbers and the monks began to stay throughout the year on their allotted place.

The first and the most important consideration for selecting the place to build *ārāmas* or *vihāras* was the source of water. The next important thing was that it would be near villages and towns so that the monks could easily approach the people for alms. Thus the *vihāras* were built mainly near perennial sources of water supply and near villages or towns. At the beginning, the *vihāra* had a simple structure. With the development of *sangha,* there was a necessity of space. To fulfil the requirement, various structures were added. The foremost was the congregational hall or meeting hall for the *uposatha*. Gradually, several buildings were added to the *vihāras* making it a huge complex. Also architectural designs were introduced. The *cullavagga* mentions various buildings that make a *vihāra*. They include *parivenas* (cell or private chambers), *koṭṭhaka* (gate chambers or porches), *upatthanasala* (service halls), *aggisala* (hall with fireplaces), *kappiyakuṭī* (storehouse outside the *vihāra*), *vachcha-kuṭī* (privies), *chankama* (promenade), *udapāna* (wells), *udapānaśālā* (sheds attached to wells), *janta-ghara* (bathrooms), *janatagharasala* (hall attached to a bathroom), *pokkharaṇī* (tank) and *maṇḍapas* (halls).

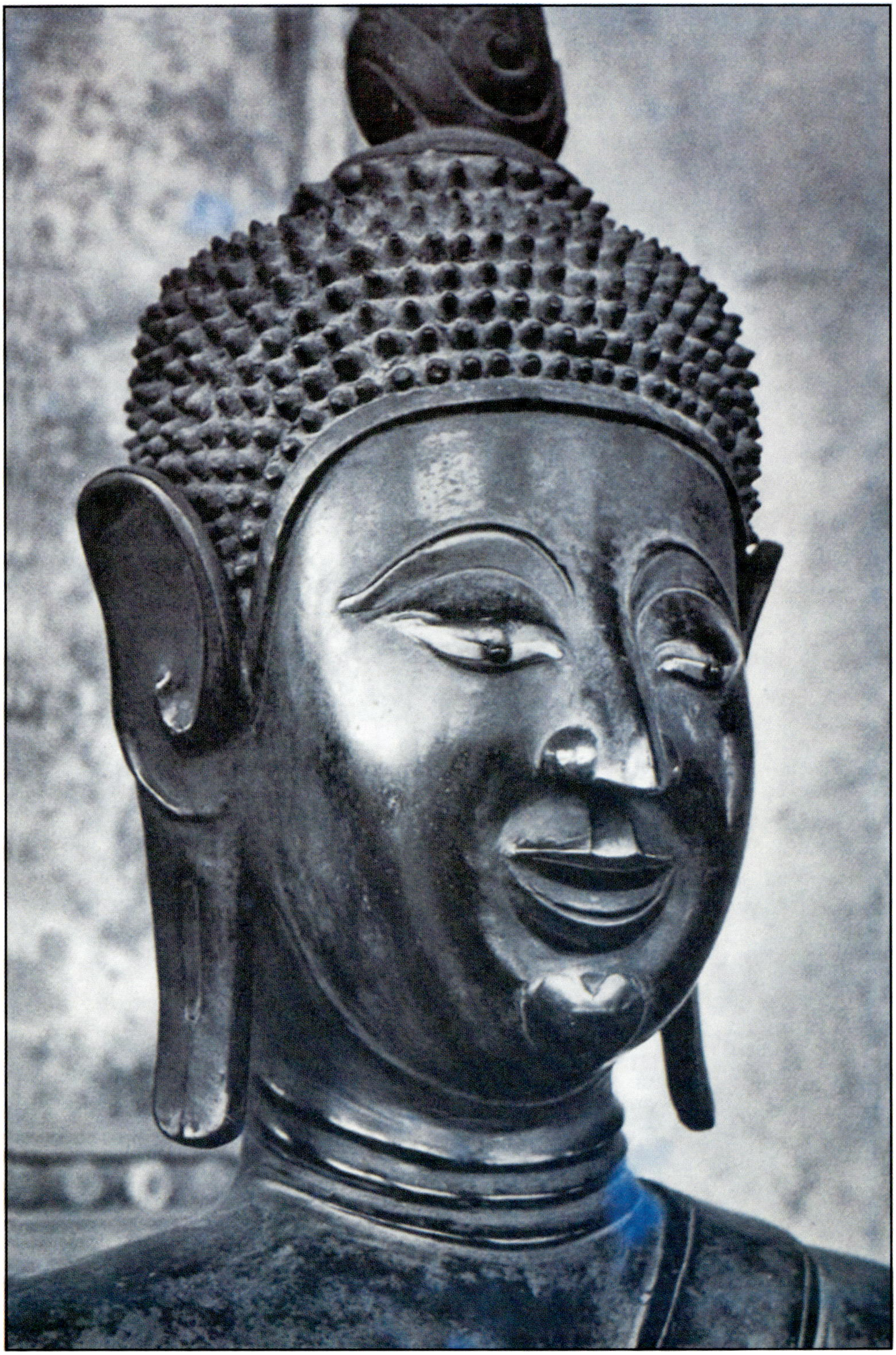

Pl. 9.7. Buddha head, bronze, Laotian art style, 18th century AD, Vat Ho Phra Kheo, Vientiane.

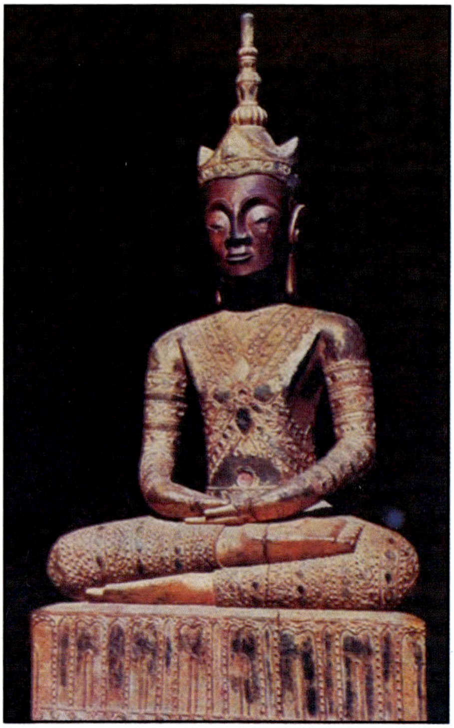

Pl. 9.8. Buddha in meditation, provincial Laotian art style, 18th century AD, found in north-west of Laos, Vat Phra Keo Museum, Vientiane.

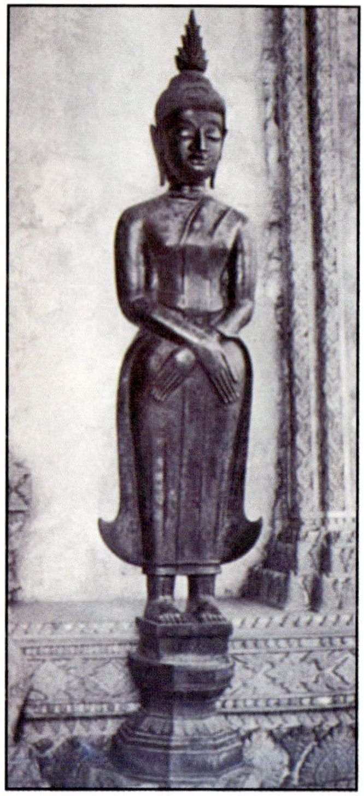

Pl. 9.9. Standing bronze Buddha image, late Laotian art style, 18th century AD, found at Vat Phra Kheo, Vientiane.

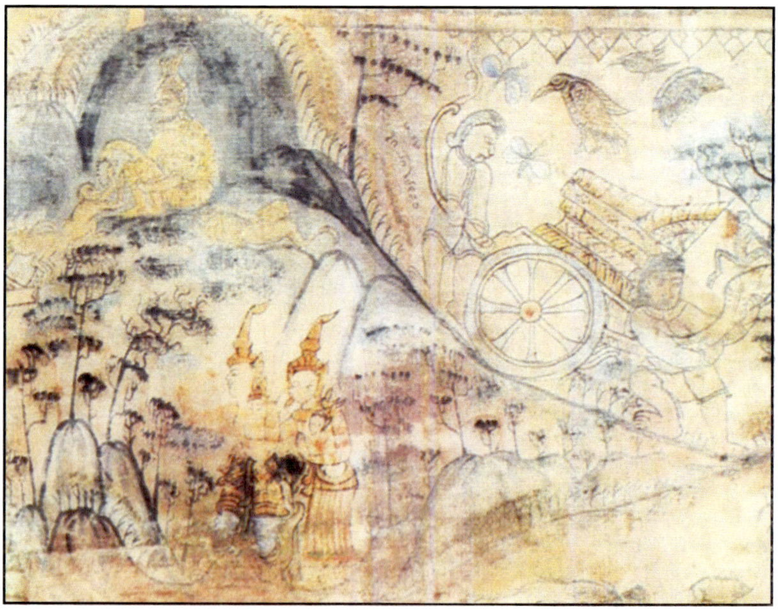

Pl. 9.10. Fragment of a wall painting showing *JÂtaka* story, first-half of the 19th century AD, Vientiane.

The concept of *vihāras* in Laos was derived from India but their architectural style was quite different from the Indian style. It was made with a view to suit the climatic conditions of the area. In Laos, old *vihāras* are rarely present in their original form. However, Vat Sisaket in Vientiane retains its original appearance. At Luang Prabang, many *vihāras* were built during 17th and 18th centuries. They still stand but have lost their original form as they have been restored and rebuilt many times and often enlarged. Therefore, their original artistic features cannot be traced.

The architectural plans of the Laotian *vihāras* were designed very scientifically. Its style has close similarity with the Thai architecture. No doubt, during the Sukhothai period, the Laotian architectural plans faced various changes and culminated into a unique structure.

The Laotian *vihāra* is a rectangular building. It contains an altar on which the image of the Buddha is placed. The architectural style varies from place to place. In the cooler climatic areas like northern Laos, the buildings have to be enclosed and are therefore covered by huge roofs overhanging on very low walls as in Vat Kong in Xieng Khouang and Vat Xieng Thong in Luang Prabang. In the warmer areas like southern Laos, provision of sufficient ventilation is given. The general outline has a more upward momentum, the walls are higher and the roofs proportionately less important. The porches are generally built at the front of the sanctuaries facing the altar.

The building of the *vihāra*, generally, consists of a nave flanked either by aisles or surrounded by a gallery to which access is gained through one or two porches. The construction plans of the buildings of the *vihāras* are of two types. In the first type, the building is constructed on each side of the median axis of the nave which is sometimes flanked by aisles separated from it by pillars. The altar is set at the end of the nave against the back wall. The sanctuaries built according to this plan have saddle-shaped roofs, often tiers. In the second type, the circumambulatory gallery surrounds the nave on all four sides and the altar is generally in the last section of the main body of the *vihāra*. A small raised roof covers the nave, and there is a lean-to roof on all four sides above the gallery.[21] The example of this type of sanctuary is Vat Viṣṇu in Luang Prabang.

Adjoining the *vihāra,* there are also other buildings such as the library, meeting rooms for the devotees, etc. Some of these buildings are built entirely of masonry and have a corbelled roof with lights in it and a doorway in the shape of the ace of spades. Some of the Lao miniature *vihāras* are without side aisles or galleries. The library of the *vihāras* has a small building in the shape of an inverted, truncated pyramid which houses manuscript chest. There are two in Vientiane, at Vat In Peng and Vat Sisaket; the latter is strongly influenced by Burmese architecture. In southern Laos, the meeting rooms for the devotees are big and nicely built.

## *STŪPA (THAṬ)*

Among the Buddhist monuments, the *stūpa* is an important relic. Its value and concept developed in different times. The *stūpa* as a religious object was adopted and sanctified by the Buddha himself as his Truth Body (*Dharmakāya*). Even Buddha proclaimed that Arhats, Bodhisattvas and Tathagatas are worthy of *stūpas,* and that whoever may pay respects and understand this significance will experience furtherance in their minds. The concept of *stūpa* was later changed from a monument of the dead into a monument for the living. Over the course of time, more and more religious and spiritual values were added to it, so that it eventually was considered a miniature of the entire cosmos. The *stūpas* were built wherever Buddhism flourished, but their shape and architectural style varied from country to country. The *stūpa* is called *thaṭ* in Laotian language.

The Buddhist texts mention different types of stūpas. But generally eight types of *stūpas* are found: 1. Enlightenment: it has a flight of four perfect square steps which are free from embellishments, although there is a tradition of making all the upper edges of the steps bulge but by one-quarter of their own height to have an attractive look. 2. Heaped Lotuses also called as Auspicious Appearance and Appearance of Sugata: it comprises a flight of four circular steps adorned with heaped lotuses. There is also a tradition of making a maximum of seven steps to symbolise the seven paces that the Gautam Buddha took immediately after his birth in the Lumbani garden of Kapilavastu. 3. Multiple Auspicious Doors also called as Divine Wisdom: it comprises a flight of four square steps and each side's centre bulges out by one-third the size of their width. These stūpas have 108 doors or niches at the maximum, 56 in the medium and sixteen in minimum. Symbolically, four doors on each side symbolise the four noble truths, eight doors on each side symbolise the eight doors of liberation, twelve doors on each side symbolise the twelve links of interdependent origination and sixteen doors on each side symbolise the sixteen types of emptiness. 4. The Great Miracle or Conquest of Tirthikas: it is identical to the preceding ones (having a flight of four square steps projected in their centre), although it does not have doors or niches on the steps and is devoid of further embellishments. 5. Descent from Heaven or alternatively named Offered by Devas: the structural formation of this *stūpa* is also similar to the preceding ones, but it has three ladders in the centre of each side's projected area. 6. Reconciliation: it comprised four octagonal steps formed by cutting off the four corners of the flight of four steps to form eight even sides. They are free from all embellishments. Occasionally, though rarely, there is a tradition of making all the upper edges of the steps projected out by one-third of their own height. 7. Victory: it has three circular steps rather than four. Even the base of ten-virtues and the vase-base are circular. 8. Niravana: it is a unique type *stūpa* because of its bell-shaped dome in which the mouth rests directly on the base of ten-virtues without any steps.[22]

Built of masonry, the Laotian *thaṭ* is virtually a solid structure. Inside the structure, sacred relics of Buddha including the texts on the laws of Buddhism were housed. Some of the Laotian *thaṭ* were made over the ashes of the dead of the holy persons. The principal Laotian *thaṭ* is built behind the *vihāra;* other less important *thaṭs* are in the courtyard.

In Laos, various architectural shapes of the *stūpas* are found. It is because of the influence of Khmer and Thai architecture. The main part, *anda,* of That Mak Mo at Vat Viṣṇu has hemispherical shaped Sri Lanka type *stūpa*. Some Laotian *stūpas* have a bell-shaped *anda* as in Thai's Sukhothai style. The Khmer influenced *stūpa* is That Luang in Vientiane. It has the tower (*prasat*) of Khmer temple architecture, square plan, redented at the corners, and niche on each side containing an image of the Buddha. The most characteristics shape of the superstructure of *thaṭ* is the bulbous spire.

Some of the *stūpas* have complex architectural plan revealing symbolism. The That Luang's quadripartite dome *anda* is surmounted by a bulbous spire surrounded at the base by lotus petals; it rests on three-tiered square plinth. The three terraces symbolise the *Traiphum,* the three worlds of Buddhist cosmology: the world of desire, appearance and formless. Thirty tiny reliquary buildings, built on the top of the terrace, evoke the perfections of the Buddha and surround the *anda,* which represents the attainment of final liberation from the cycle of rebirths by the Buddha (*mahāparinirvāṇa*).

## PAGODA

During earlier times, a large number of pagodas were built in Laos. Francis Garnier,[23] in his exploration work, has reported the ruins of several pagodas[24] at Se Cong, on the right bank of Mekong River. One of the abandoned pagodas had old brick towers hidden amidst leaves. Three of them were still standing: two rather big ones in a dilapidated condition; the other one, some sort of sanctuary barely five to six metres high, was better preserved. From the architecture point of view, the sanctuary was superb in refinement and perfection.

The edifice consisted of four thick walls above which towered in a type of truncated pyramid forming a staircase and which formerly must have ended in a gilded spire. The walls were adorned with bases, pilasters, frescos and fine and elegant cornices. The sanctuary had two very delicately worked garlands, one composed of flowers, the other of birds with spread wings. All this was made of cast bricks of the best quality that were generally found in the old ruins of Laos. Even nowadays, the Laotians construct their pagodas elegantly and artistically tapered, curved with elevated roofs and their thousand and one ornaments.

## DECORATIVE STYLE OF THE RELIGIOUS BUILDINGS

The Laotians decorate their religious buildings elegantly. The principal media of the decorations are stucco, and guilded carved wood, glass inlay and wall paintings. The roof-ridges are set off by lentils and half-way along the main ridge is a group of finial that evokes Mount Meru, the axis of the world in Hindu and Buddhist cosmology, surrounded by seven cosmic mountains. The sloping gables of the saddle-shaped roofs are decorated with the bodies of the *nāgas* (the serpent king), the head of which are raised at the lower end with the tail meeting above the gable-top. The pediments are divided into panels or carved wood, which is sometimes gilded.

The window panels of *vihāras* and *uposathas* are generally decorated with carving of figures. In Luang Prabang, the Vat Nang's doors have nice floral decoration. Both the doors have the image of a same styled woman. The images are probably of a king and are shown standing on a lion's head similar to the lion capital of Aśoka at Sarnath. Such a decorative style has similarity with pre-Gupta art style of India.

## PAINTINGS

The painting techniques were known to the Laotians since the foundation of their mighty kingdom, Lan Xang. The Laotian style of painting evolved during 15th to 17th centuries AD when the glory of Lan Xang kingdom was at its zenith. The aesthetic sense, principles and styles of religious art remained unchanged till the 20th century AD.

The Laotian paintings are available as illustrations of palm leaves manuscripts, the paintings on the walls of the monasteries and temples, paintings on doors and shutters in the temples. So far as the mural paintings are concerned, there is hardly any painting before the latter half of the 19th century owing to the climatic condition of the country. These paintings are on the interior walls of the temple and on the facades where these are protected by a porch.

The painters have illustrated their subjects either from the episodes from the life of the Buddha and the previous life of Buddha (Pl. 9.10) described in *Jātakas* or epic scenes from Thai and Lao versions of the Rāmāyaṇa. The wall painting of the temple Vat Pa Hwak in Luang Prabang is exceptional one. Although, badly damaged, it depicts *Jambūpatisūtra*, the conversion of Prince Jambūpatī. The painting on the walls of Vat Pa Ka temple, also in Luang Prabang, is in traditional style. The scenes are taken from the Thai version of the Rāmāyaṇa, the *Rāmakien*. At Vat Up Mong temple, in Vientiane, the paintings illustrate the scenes of the Lao version of the Rāmāyaṇa, the *Phra Lăk Phra Lām* and are painted in popular Laotian style. A Laotian painting made on cloth of the first half of the 19th century reveals the traditional style.[25] It is a horizontal panel narrating the story of Prince Pabet in sequence. The entire story of Prince Pabet is based on the *Jātaka* story. It is invariably hung on the walls of the temple sanctuary at the entrance of the portico. The narrative of the painting covers a wide panorama of Laotian life including images of village huts and of palaces, birds, animals, water, day-to-day scences of festivals. The traditional Lao paintings are heavily Influenced by Thai paintings. The later phase of paintings, no doubt, reveals the Chinese influence. Since Independence, Laotian painters, even those trained in western technique at the Vientiane School of Art, have increasingly sought inspiration from Lao subjects.

The technique of wall paintings, no doubt, was adopted from the Thais.[26] The wall painting by stencilling gold leaf onto lacquer is a distinguishing feature of Laotian painter. Through this technique, the Laotian painters have shown native depictions of Buddhist scenes. The black or red lacquered background on the paintings of the the roofs, wall surfaces, beams, columns, wooden doors and shutters of the temples testify the efficiency of the painters in mixing the colours in lac. Their presentation of various episodes on natural scenes reveals high level of aesthetic sense.

## CONCLUSION

The sculptural and architectural remains reveal the fact that Buddhist art of Laos bloomed into a beautiful art style after passing through various stages. The Khmer artists gave it a distinct shape. The refinements in the art were contributed by the various schools of Thai art. The Burmese gave it the final touch. But the sculptures are based on Gupta and post-Gupta style of Indian art. The sacred iconographic elements were always retained. The *mahāpuruṣa lakṣanaṁ* have always been reflected in each and every sculpture. The sculptures were carved mostly in the postures of the *bhūmisparśa mudrā* and *dhyāna mudra*. In the latter stage, the images are shown full face, with a subtle smile, sharp heavy nose and globular eyes surmounted by distinctively incised arched eyebrows.

## NOTES AND REFERENCES

1. Henri Mouhot, *Diary: Travels in the Central Parts of Siam, Cambodia and Laos during the Years 1858-61,* abridged and edited by Christopher Pym, London, 1966.
2. Perala Ratnam, *Laos and Its Culture,* 1982.
3. G. Coedés, "An Introduction to the History of Laos" (in) Rene de Berval, *Kingdom of Laos,* Saigon, 1959, p. 23.
4. V. Fausboll (ed.), *Samuddavāṇija Jātaka* no. 466 (in) *The Jātaka,* IV, pp. 158-66; H.B. Sarkar quotes this passage in "Bengal and her Traffic Routes in the Bay of Bengal and South-East Asia," *JAS,* XIV/1, p. 86.
5. V. Trenckner, *The Milindapanho,* p. 359.
6. Perala Ratnam, *op. cit.,* p. 66.
7. T. Guignard, "Note Historique Et ethnographique sur le Laos et les Thay", *Revue Indochinoise,* I, 1904, p. 236.
8. Donald P. Whitaker, *et al., Laos: Country Study,* pp. 27-28.
9. B.J. Terwiel, *The Tai of Assam and Ancient Tai Ritual,* I (Life-Cycle Ceremonies), pp. 10-11.
10. G.H. Luce, "The Early Syam in Burma's History", *JSS,* 1958, pp. 59-101.
11. B.J. Terwiel, *op. cit.,*p. 11.
12. Arthur J. Dommen, *Laos: Keystone of Indochina,* p. 10.
13. Donald P. Whitaker, *et al., op. cit.,* p. 29.
14. G. Coedés, *op. cit.,* p. 20.
15. *Ibid.,* p. 21.
16. M.C. Subhadradis Diskul, *Art of Thailand: A Brief History,* Bangkok, 1991, p. 4.
17. *Ibid.,* p. 7.
18. G. Coedés, "Le Site de Janapada", *BEFEO,* XLII, p. 8.
19. G. Coedés, *The Indianized States of South-East Asia,* pp. 99-100.

20. Louis Frederic, *The Art of South-East Asia (Temple and Sculpture)*, pp. 403-4.
21. Pema Dorjee, *Stupa and Its Technology: A Tibeto-Buddhist Perspective*, Delhi, pp. 50-61.
22. Jane Turner, *Dictionary of Art*, 18, p. 765.
23. Francis Garnier, *Travels in Cambodia and Parts of Laos: The Mekong Exploration Commission Report (1866-1868)*, I, Bangkok, 1996, p. 158.
24. Several ruins of pagodas are found in Laos. It is because when Laotians abandon a pagoda, they never repair it. It is left to fall totally into ruins. The Laotians consider such places very sacred and leave them in isolation. Usually the Laotians make a detour in order to not disturb the solitude of the monument believing that the spirits frequently visit such places.
25. N.A. Gozheva, G.M. Sorokina and others, *Art of Indochina*, Moscow, 1991, pp. 38-45 (in Russian).
26. M. Giteau, "Lao Painting" (in) *The Dictionary of Art*, edited by Jane Turner, 18, p. 770.

# 10

# Rāmāyaṇa in Laotian Art

Induja Awasthi

Laos is a small country in South-East Asia situated on the eastern bank of the mighty Mekong River, bounded on all four sides by Thailand, Cambodia, Vietnam, Burma (Myanmar) and also China. The kingdom of Lan Xang (old name for Laos) was in existence in the middle of the 14th century. Later this area came under colonial rule. At the end of second World War, the colonial rule came to an end and four states namely Laos, Thailand, Cambodia and Vietnam emerged as self-governing countries.

This entire region has had strong cultural ties with India since centuries. Thus the culture of Laos is made up of early form of Hinduism and Theravada Buddhism; it has deep philosophic aspect of Buddhism mixed with rich literary aspect of Hinduism. Thus the Rāmāyaṇa—principal text of the Hindus—came to be a part of the living tradition of Laos.

The Rāmāyaṇa became part of the Laotian art in all its aspects, performing as well as plastic. Laotian paintings, dance, drama, music and its sculpture and architecture all became permeated by Rāmāyaṇa. It is also interesting that in Laos, the literary, performing and plastic arts are so inter-related that the Rāmāyaṇa paintings on the temple walls and scenes and setting of the dance and drama seem to be reflection of each other.

Laotian art is comparatively new. The scholars place it earliest in the 18th century and also it has been less studied. The influences from its immediate neighbours specially Thailand and Burma are unmistakably to be found. In spite of the diverse influences, Laotian art has preserved its originality; hence its study is important in the context of South-East Asian art.

As has been said, Rāmāyaṇa has been the major subject for the different art forms in Laos. Mural and temple sculptures and carvings as well as music, dance and drama are all Rāmāyaṇa-oriented.

There are several versions of Rāmāyaṇa in Laos. The manuscripts of larger version namely *Phra Lăk Phra Lām* was found in the royal museum in Laotian language which was published by Sachchidanand Sahai in 1973 (now the translation in English has also been published). It is believed to be written by monk Dhuttaphochau (also named as Buddha-Ghosacharya) during the first half of the 19th century. It portrays Rāma as a mighty king—the author who was also the court poet has described Rāma (or his king?) marching against and gaining victory on certain part of Thailand and founding some cities on his way back. The city of Ayudhya which the Thais believe and preserve as their ancient capital is mentioned to be founded by Rāma and Lakshman. It seems likely that to sing the glory of his own king and to give popularity and performance to his writing, he wrote this Lao version of the Rāmāyaṇa which was already known and popular among the people and in the name of Rāma described achievements of his own king.

The other version *Gvāy Dvóṟaḥbī* was also published by Sahai in 1976—the manuscripts of which was preserved in Royal Palace of Luang Prabang. The name of this version is based on the buffalo episode. The fight of Valin with buffalo Dvóṟaḥbī must be popular in that region, that is why the Rāmāyaṇa has been named on such a small episode. *Gvāy Dvóṟaḥbī* provides unique example of adapting an Indian story to local habits and customs. In this version, folkloric elements have been introduced perhaps to bring it nearer to people. Laotian Rāmāyaṇa versions have numerous innovations from the original. In the Laotian Rāmāyaṇa, Lakshman is more important than Rāma as is evident by the title of the text *Phra Lăk Phra Lām*. Rāvaṇa does not have ten heads and twenty hands but he is a handsome prince who has special favour from Indra so much so that Indra helps in abduction of Sīta by turning himself into the golden deer (Marich episode is absent). Hanumān is shown as Rāma's son. Sīta is the daughter of Rāvaṇa. Later, Sīta is thrown out into the ocean after learning from the astrologer that she is inauspicious for her father.

Innovation of the story can be seen in the murals also. The murals have significant differences from the literary version. The murals only portray the story up to Rāma's victory over Lanka whereas in the literary versions, the banishment of Sīta and birth of twin sons are described in detail. The Valin-Sugriva duo also have reverse roles. Sugriva is shown as the elder brother and Valin the younger one.

An interesting point which is common in all the South-East Asian countries is that the Rāmāyaṇa frescos are found in the Buddhist temples (Vat Ka Pe and Vat Mai in Luang Prabang) and *vihāras* (Vat Oup Moung in Vientiane). This is because the Lao people believe that Rāma is Bodhisattava (Buddha in previous birth) and therefore painting the Rāmāyaṇa scenes became part of the worship of the monks.

The paintings on the walls of Vat Ka Pe and Vat Mai are based on *Phra Lăk Phra Lām*. Vat Mai was built by King Anurut in 1796. Its roof is laid on a beautifully carved wooden pillar decorated with wooden planks on which stories from the Rāmāyaṇa namely stories of Hanumān's mother and Rāvaṇa's birth are carved. Vat Pa Ke was built in 1851 by Prince Chautrat, its door panels are decorated with the images of goddess Parvati and Durga riding the Lion. The well-lacquered roofs and walls are decorated by gilded painting showing various episodes from the Rāmāyaṇa.

Another temple in Luang Prabang, is Vat Viṣṇu decorated with sculptures and carvings of the Viṣṇu, Śiva, Brahmā and Indra in its four doors. Viṣṇu is shown as riding Garuḍa and holding conch, *chakra* (disc), mane and lotus in his four hands; Brahmā sitting on a lotus, Indra on his elephant Airawat and Śiva on his Nandi Bull. Nandi is depicted as having horns like a bull but his mouth appears to be a horse's mouth. The reason of this mistake is the absence of cows and oxen in Laos. The inside walls and roofs of the temple have paintings of Hanumān, Rāma and Rāvaṇa's fight. The images of other Hindu gods, goddesses and *yakṣhas* have also been painted.

The well-known Buddhist monastry in Vientiane, Vat Oup Moung, is also distinguished by the Rāmāyaṇa scenes. Murals, based on *Gvāy Dvóṟaḥbī,* can be seen on the interior walls of the *vihāra*. Because of the poor quality of paint and no effort for preservation, these paintings have faded. The painter has painted the Rāmāyaṇa in the background of Lao culture and life style. Lao people, their costumes and ornaments, house and household articles, have been vividly painted.

The Rāmāyaṇa dance and drama have gorgeous colourful costumes, masks, beautiful headdresses and crown and music very similar to Thai and Cambodian Rāmāyaṇa dance and drama. This is very popular and whenever it is presented in festivals and religious occasions, there is a large appreciative audience. Performers come from all the societies and feel proud to take part in the Rāmāyaṇa dance and drama. The troupe is maintained by the court and proper instructions and rehearsals continuously go on in Luang Prabang. In Vientiane, the Nāṭyaśālā, financed by the government, gives training to the artistes of Rāmāyaṇa dance and drama.

With all the similarities with the other South-East Asian arts, Laos has its originality. The paintings, the dance, the drama and the architecture are essentially Laotian. The artists, painters, sculptors and architects have developed their own style which makes their art unique.

The story of Laotian art cannot be complete without mentioning the beautiful architecture and sculptures. The entire region is full of temples, dedicated to Buddha, decorated with pictures of Hindu gods and goddesses. There is a wide variety of designs of the *stūpas* and *vihans* (*vihāras*) which have also different styles. Beautiful door panels, showing the images of Hindu gods and goddesses, were carved and lacquered. The columns of the *vihāras* are beautifully carved. The Muang designs of candle holders are, of course, the images of Buddha in various poses like Māravijaya, walking Buddha and Mahāparinirvāṇa but all these belong in the temples full of Rāmāyaṇa paintings. Therefore, it will be pertinent to say that Laotian art is mainly and predominantly centred on the Rāmāyaṇa which is the life-blood of Laotian people.

# 11

# The Mural Paintings of Laos

Neeru Misra

The topographic location of Laos is mountainous, covering ninety per cent of the entire country. The northern section of the mountainous range is heavily forested whereas the southern section contains limestone terraces with comparatively much less vegetation. The maximum elevation is Phou Bia in the north, 2820 m (9252 ft) above sea level. In the south, heights reach about 1980 m (about 6500 ft). The Mekong River, the principal river of Laos, enters in the north-west from Thailand, flows south along the Laos-Thailand border and enters Cambodia in the south-west. The tributaries of the Mekong River in Laos rise in the mountains and flow through deep valleys.

Laos was known as Muong Xieng Thong [Laem Thong]. In the early Sanskrit texts it has been referred to as *Suvarṇabhūmi Pradesha (Souvaṇṇaphoūm Pathet)* or the Land of Gold.[1] Geographically the countries of Burma, Malaysia, Thailand, Vietnam, and Cambodia surround this country. Laos is South-East Asia's only landlocked nation. The capital and largest city of Laos is Vientiane. The total area of the country is 236,800 sq km (91,429 sq miles).[2]

The Laotian culture is closely mixed with the religion the region experienced over the years. The semblance of the cultural traditions of Laos with the Indian culture have led the scholars to conclude that it is an outpost of the Indian civilisation.[3] However, the systematic study of the Indian culture in Laos by establishing the texts which would form the basis of the study of the most popular culture form—the Rāmāyaṇa—has been a very recent one.[4] Besides the Rāmāyaṇa, the impact of Buddhism is deep and all pervading. Buddhist temples in every village also functions as the centres of formal learning and even as centres of higher education in some areas.[5] Predominantly an agricultural country, the life of the commoner is organised around religion. The daily and annual life activities are largely governed by the Buddhist calendar.[6] Luang Prabang and Vientiane are known as "Cities of a Thousand Temples" and have many examples of traditional Buddhist art and architecture. The king's palace and the That Luang Shrine, in Luang Prabang, are the most famous shrines in Laos.

The first identifiable inhabitants of what is now Laos were people known collectively as the Kha, who as early as the 5th century AD were living in the country under the suzerainty of the state of Funan. They subsequently came under the domination of the kingdom of Chenla, an early Khmer kingdom, and its successor state, centred at Angkor.

It is stated that "in the meantime, the Lao and other Tai peoples had been gradually penetrating south from Nanchao (in present-day Yunnan, China), supplanting the Kha. By the 12th century they had apparently established their own principalities, although much of this period remains shrouded in legend. The Lao migration received its final impetus from the Mongol destruction of Nanchao in the 13th and 14th centuries."[7]

In the mid-14th century, the Khmer king at Angkor, Jayavarman Paramesvara, married his daughter to a Lao prince, Fa Ngum, and helped him found the independent kingdom of Lan Xang ("Million Elephants"), with its capital at Muong Swa (present-day Luang Prabang). A great warrior, who earned the title 'Conqueror', united the Lao principalities and was frequently at war with both the kingdoms of Ayutthaya and Annam. Largely by the efforts of his Khmer queen, the Laos during his reign adopted Theravada Buddhism. Thus the first great Thai kingdom in Laos was that of Lan Xang founded by Fa Ngum (AD 1353-AD 1373).[8]

Fa Ngum was deposed and succeeded by his son in AD 1373, who further consolidated and organised the kingdom. In the second half of the 15th century, hostilities with Annam resulted in the fall of the capital, but the Annamese were soon driven back, and a long period of peace followed. Lan Xang's maximum extension came in the 16th century, when the Laotian king claimed and won the crown of neighbouring Chieng Mai. This, however, marked the beginning of a long struggle with the Burmese, during which the capital was moved to Vientiane. The Burmese revaged the country in 1574, and after a period of anarchy Souligna-Vongsa acceded to the throne in 1637. He established peace with his neighbours to the east and west, and his subsequent rule is considered a golden age in Laotian history.

In 1700, after Souligna-Vongsa's death, an exiled nephew of his brought in a Vietnamese force to help him seize the throne. His relatives, however, would not tolerate Vietnamese rule, and they established a separate kingdom at Luang Prabang in 1707. That was the end of Lan Xang; by 1713 Laos was split into the three states of Luang Prabang, Vientiane and Champassak.

Hostilities between Siam (Thailand) and Vientiane led to the conquering of latter in 1778, and at the same time Luang Prabang and Champassak were forced to acknowledge Siamese suzerainty. When Vientiane tried to assert its independence in 1827, Siamese force completely destroyed it.

During the second half of the 19th century, the French began to make their presence felt. A French military expedition in 1893 occupied the most important towns of the country and forced the Siamese to recognise the protectorate that France had established over Laotian territory east of the Mekong River. In 1904, France obtained whatever Laotian territory had remained under Siamese control. The French ruled indirectly through the king of Luang Prabang and a hierarchy of royal officials, although the French Resident supervisor always had the final word.

During World War II (1939-45) the Japanese occupied Indo-China. When they withdrew, an independence movement known as the Lao Issarak ("Free Laos") formed a nationalist government, which collapsed when the French reoccupied the region in 1946. The French then signed an agreement with the king of Luang Prabang that established him as king of a unified Laos within the French Union. A constitution providing for an elected legislature was promulgated on May 11, 1947. In 1949 Laos became an independent state within the French Union, and most of the nationalist leaders, who had fled at the time of the French reoccupation, returned to the country. A few dissidents under the leadership of Prince Souphanouvong, however, allied themselves with the pro-Communist Vietminh forces fighting the French in Vietnam. These Laotians, called the Pathet Lao ("Lao State"), joined with the Vietminh forces to invade Laos in April 1953 and quickly gained control of large areas. Later that year, the French agreed to give Laos full independence.

Eminent historian A.L. Basham in his famous book, *The Wonder that was India* states that "The whole of South-East Asia received most of its culture from India, early in the 5th century BC."[9] Subsequently, many highly civilised kingdoms became instrumental in spreading Hinduism and Buddhism to this part of the globe. As a result, Valmiki's Rāmāyaṇa and many other mythological versions of Indian religion travelled to South-East Asia.

The culture of Laos is very close to that of Thailand.[10] During the colonial period, this area was also known as the Indo-China region. Laos has visible influence of early Hindu period and Theravada Buddhism. The synthesis of both the religions in a profound aesthetic manner is reflected in their temples, sculptures, and mural paintings. The study of these paintings clearly shows the changes and modifications made in the Rāmāyaṇa stories. In a way they represent indigenous folk-tales with some fragments of the great epic of all times, the Rāmāyaṇa.

According to Mahasila Viravong, the word Lao means civilised or big.[11] The social and political history of the region gave strength to this country to rise sometime in the late 13th century. This also gave an expression to its religion, art and culture, which remained influenced by the Rāmāyaṇa, Brahmanical and Buddhist philosophy, which came from its neighbouring areas. The Rāmāyaṇa gave numerous artistic styles and Buddhism brought the society into moral codes and certain amount of discipline. Thus, Laos provides the artistic flavour of pre-Buddhist Hindu art, Buddhist art and Brahmanical art superimposed on different versions of the Rāmāyaṇa.

The Laotian art forms of the early period can be divided into four parts—the paintings, the sculpture in the temple architecture, dance and the manuscripts or writing of sacred texts. Out of these, the paintings have been the most preferred medium of communicating the religious themes to the devout. Laotian manuscripts are on palm leaves and some of these, that have survived, are a rich treasure of fine calligraphy with occasional illustrations.[12] The paintings—on the walls, doors and shutters of the temples—are several in numbers and give us a deep insight into this art form of the region.[13]

Pictorial representations not only had a greater reach but were also understandable to the illiterate majority. The antiquity of the mural paintings in Laos is mainly found in the Royal Palace or Luang Prabang, in the walls of the Vat Pa Ke temple and in the province of Vientiane at the Vat Oup Moung. The Vientiane version of the Rāmāyaṇa is different from the Indian version[14] and known as *Phra Lăk Phra Lām* (Beloved Lakshman Beloved Rāma), it is not the translation of any of the then known texts of the peninsula.[15]

The medium of Laotian paintings is either polychrome or gold leaf stencilled on a dull red or black background.[16] Most of these mural paintings on the walls of the temples are still protected. However, the pictorial presentations on the facades, even though protected by the porches, have over the period of time, due to the vagaries of nature, faded and the base of dry plaster has also flaked.

The subjects and themes of these mural paintings cover a vast range of episodes and life of Buddha, his previous lives as narrated in the *Jātakas* and the scenes from the South Asian versions of the Rāmāyaṇa.

The Royal Palace is built on the banks of river Mekong [Ma Gaṅgā or the Mother Ganges]. It is a city of temples. There are approximately 41 Vats or temples adorned by several mural paintings on the themes from the Rāmāyaṇa.

At Vientiane, in the Vat Oup Muong, all the paintings are done with watercolours on the walls of the main Chamber hall. It is mainly a Buddhist monastery containing narration of indigenous stories from the life of Rāma. As per the version of H. Deydier, over two and a half dozen scenes are artistically handled on the walls of the central hall.[17] The name of the artist is stated to be Thit Panh.

The life of Buddha has been depicted mainly on the upper parts of the walls. The lower parts of the walls of the corridors, bays and doorways have been used to paint the *Jātakas*. Of these, the theme of the *Vessantara Jātaka* has been used fairly profusely. Several dilapidated paintings at Vat Pa Hwak in Luang Prabang depict the conversion of Prince Jambūpati based on the narration of *Jambūpatisūtra*. The scheme of colours matches the grandeur of the theme dealt with in the story of *Jambūpatisūtra*.

Scenes from the Thai version of the Rāmāyaṇa, the *Rāmakien*, have been used to decorate the walls at Vat Pa Ke also at Luang Prabang. Over the years, the colours have lost their sheen.

The Lao version of the Rāmāyaṇa also known as *P'a Lăk P'a Lām* is illustrated at Vat Up Mong in Vientiane. The execution of these paintings is in the popular style.

The paintings of Laos have a great deal of Thai influence. However, at the same time, the depiction of the guardian figures has been done with the Chinese influence and some scholars yet feel that the treatment of the landscape has the influence of the West.

Very few paintings were produced during the period of French colonialism [1893-1947], and most of these are the portraits of the officials in the western style.

The technique of Laotian paintings exhibits a clear influence of Thai art.[18] The scenes from Buddha's life are painted with stencilled gold leaf on lacquer. Sometimes, gold-leaf stencil work has been used on black and red background.[19] This type of decoration is mainly found on the beams, wooden doors, shutters of the temples, and on the surfaces of the walls. In 1959-75, King Savang Vatthana deputed Thao Sin Kaeo, an artist, to restore the damaged paintings in the Red Chapel of the Vat Xieng Thong in Luang Prabang. During modern period, at some places, new illustrations from the *Jātaka* stories have also been undertaken.

The Laotians also believe that Buddha is the reincarnation of Rāma. Therefore, the paintings are amalgamated in these two subject matters. Some parts of the paintings preserved at Vat Oup Mong at Vientiane are already discussed in some detail in this paper.

## NOTES AND REFERENCES

1. Dhanit Yupho, *Suvarṇabhūmi*, Bangkok, 1967; Lokesh Chandra and Perala Ratnam, *Studies in Indo-Asian Art and Culture,* Vol. 5, New Delhi, International Academy on Indian Culture, 1977, p. 183.
2. "Laos", *Microsoft Encarta 97 Encyclopaedia.* © 1993-1996 Microsoft Corporation.
3. Rene De Berval, *Kingdom of Laos,* Saigon, 1959, p. 23.
4. The preliminary studies of the Lao version of *Rāmāyaṇa* were undertaken by H. Deydier, "The Rāmāyaṇa in Laos", *JRAS*, 22; *Les Origines et La Naissance de Ravana dans le Rāmāyaṇa Laotien, BEFEO,* 44; Vo Thu Tinh, "Phra Lăk Phra Lām", *BARL,* 6, 1971, pp. 1-94.
5. Perala Ratnam, *Laos and its Culture,* New Delhi, Tulsi Publishing House, 1982, pp. 24-25.
6. Buddhism came in this region much before the 3rd century BC before the time of Aśoka. Many contemporary literary sources state that only seven weeks after his Enlightenment, Buddha had sent his two disciples to the area of Indo-China peninsula. Promsak Jermsawtdi, *Thai Art with Indian Influences,* New Delhi, Abhinav Publications, 1979, p. 23. For details of the impact of Buddhism in the region see Luand Boribal Buribhand, *Pravatisat Pra Putasasana Nai Pratethai (The History of Buddhism in Thailand),* Bangkok, Chatra Press, 1955; Saeng Monavitoon, *Sasanawongsa or History of Religion,* Bangkok, 1963; Siridham, *Karnapoklaong Kanasong nai Yukboran thuang Yukpatchuban Pak I (The Administration of Buddhist Samgha from Ancient to Present Times, Part I*), Bangkok, Yungli Press, 1933; P.V. Bapat, *2500 Years of Buddhism,* New Delhi, Publication Division, Ministry of Information and Broadcasting, 1971.
7. "Laos", *Microsoft Encarta 97 Encyclopaedia.* © 1993-1996 Microsoft Corporation.
8. Bernard Philippe Groslier, *Indo-China: Art in the Melting Pot of Races,* London, Metheun, 1962, p. 223.
9. A.L. Basham, *The Wonder that was India,* New Delhi, pp. 1-4.
10. Sachchidanand Sahai, *Rāmāyaṇa in Laos: A Study in the Gvāy Dvóraḥbī,* New Delhi, B.R. Publishing Corporation, 1976.
11. Perala Ratnam, *op. cit.,* p. 97.

12. Jane Turner, ed., *The Dictionary of Art*, Kettle to Leath art, Vol. 16, Macmillan Publishers, 1996.
13. Jane Turner, *op. cit.*, p. 770.
14. The five differences between the *Lava* and the classical *Rāmāyaṇa* of Valmiki as enumerated by Lokesh Chandra and Perala Ratnam are:
    1. In *Rāmāyaṇa* of Laos, Rāma is given very non-important and subordinate role compared to the original;
    2. The true hero of the story is Rāvaṇa who is not a demon with ten heads and twenty arms as in Valmiki's text, but a clever and well read young man of great beauty and charm enjoying the protection of Indra;
    3. Sīta is the daughter of Rāvaṇa and is not totally averse to the charms of the King of Laṅka. She too has a comparatively short and unimportant role;
    4. Hanumān is the son of Rāma who leaves his monkey skin in the end of the story; and
    5. All the characters carry out their activities in Lao language and in the matter practised in Laos even today, *op. cit.*, p. 190.
15. P.B. Lafont, P'a Lăk P'a Lām, École Française d'Extréme-Orient, 6, 1957. "P.B. Lafont's summary refers to the two versions of the *Rāmāyaṇa* found in Laos. One is known as P'a Lăk P'a Lām discovered in the province of Vientiane and Pommachak (*Brahmachakra*) discovered in Muongsing, a province in the upper Meking region of North Laos. *Brahmachakra* is the Thai and Lava name for Rāvaṇa, although based on Indian version of *Rāmāyaṇa* of Valmiki. P'a Lăk P'a Lām is not a translation of any Indian work. It is an original recension belonging to the Lava people which enjoys immense popularity". Kamla Ratnam, "The Rāmāyaṇa (in) Laos" in Perala Ratnam, *Laos and its Culture,* New Delhi, Tulsi Publishing House, pp. 64-95.
16. Jane Turner, *op. cit.*, p. 770.
17. Sachchidanand Sahai, *op. cit.*, p. 75.
18. "The style and technique of Thai paintings have the basic elements of all Asian painting—with no shadows and timeless....The composition of painting is a combination of mass and line." Promsak Jermsawtdi, *Thai Art with Indian Influences,* New Delhi: Abhinav Publications, 1979.
19. Elizabeth Lyons, *Art of Bangkok Period,* Bangkok, 1968.

# Bibliography

1


Bayard, D., "The Roots of Indo-Chinese Civilisation: Recent Developments in the Prehistory of South-East Asia", *Pacific Affairs,* 53/1, 1980, pp. 89-114.

Bellwood, P., *Man's Conquest of the Pacific,* New York, 1979.

——, *Prehistory of the Indo-Malaysian Archipelago,* Sydney, 1985.

Casparis, J.G. de, *India and Maritime South-East Asia: A Lasting Relationship,* third Sri Lanka Endowment Fund Lecture, 1983.

Ciochon, R.L. and James, J., "Land of the Cham", *Archaeology,* 45/3, 1992, pp. 52-55.

Coedés, George, *The Making of South-East Asia,* Berkeley, 1969.

Davidson, J., "Recent Archaeological Activity in Vietenam", *JHKAS,* VI, 1975, pp. 80-99.

——, "Urban Genesis in Vietnam" in R.B. Smith and W. Watson (eds.), *Early South-East Asia,* Oxford, 1979, pp. 304-314.

Dehejia, V., "Brick Temples: Origins and Development" in A.G. Poster (ed.), *From Indian Earth,* Brooklyn Museum, 1986, pp. 43-56.

Desai, D., "Social Dimensions of Art in Early India", Presidential Address, Indian History Congress, Gorakhpur, 1989-90.

Glover, I.C. and Yamagata, M., "The Origins of Cham Civilization", *Archaeology in South-East Asia,* Hong Kong, 1995.

Groslier, Bernard Philippe, *Indo-China: Art in the Melting Pot of Races,* London, Methuen, 1962.

Higham, C., *The Archaeology of Mainland South-East Asia,* Cambridge, 1989.

Jacques, C., "Funan', 'Zhenla': The Reality Concealed by these Chinese Views of Indo-China" in R.B. Smith and W. Watson (eds.), *Early South-East Asia,* Oxford, 1979, pp. 371-79.

Kempers, A.J. Bernet, "The Kettledrums of South-East Asia: A Bronze Age World and its Aftermath", *MQRSEA,* 10, 1988.

Kulke, H., "Indian Colonies: Indianization or Cultural Convergence" in H.S. Nordholt (ed.), *Onderzoek in Zuidoost Azie,* Leiden, 1990, pp. 8-32.

——, *Kings and Cults: State Formation and Legitimation in India and South-East Asia,* Delhi, 1993.

Malleret, L., *L'Archaeologie du Delta du Mekong,* Paris, 1962.

Manguin, P.Y., "South-East Asian Shipping in the Indian Ocean in the First Millennium AD" in H.P. Ray and J.F. Salles (eds.), *Tradition and Archaeology: Early Maritime Contacts in the Indian Ocean,* New Delhi, 1996.

Mukherjee, B.N., "Kharoshti and Kharoshti-Brahmi Inscriptions in West Bengal (India)", *IMB,* XXV, 1990.

Parmentier, Henri, *L'Art Khmer Primitif,* I, Paris, 1927.

Ray, H.P., *The Winds of Change: Buddhism and the Maritime Links of Early South Asia,* Delhi, 1995.

Sharma, R.S., *Indian Feudalism,* Delhi, 1980.

Smith, R.B. and Watson, W. (eds.), *Early South-East Asia,* Oxford, 1979.

Sontheimer, G.D., *Pastoral Deities in Western India,* Delhi, 1993.

Sorensen, P., "Kettledrums of Heger Type I: Some Observations" in I.C. Glover and E. Glover (eds.), *South-East Asian Archaeology 1986,* Oxford, 1990, pp. 195-200.

Tan, Ha Van, "Oc Eo: Endogenous and Exogenous Elements", *VSS,* 1-2, 1986, pp. 91-101.

Taylor, K., *The Birth of Vietnam,* California, 1983.

2

Ball, Valentine, "Stone Implements Discovered in Singhbhum", *Proceedings of the Asiatic Society of Bengal,* Calcutta, 1870.

Chakrabarti, D.K., *Archaeology of Eastern India, Chotanagpur Plateau and West Bengal,* New Delhi, Munshiram Manoharlal, 1993.

Heine-Geldern, R., "Die Asiatishe Herkunft der Siidamerikanishen Metalltechnik", *Paideuma,* Vol. 5, 1954.

Higham, Charles, *The Archaeology of Mainland South-East Asia,* Cambridge, Cambridge University Press, 1989.

Imam, Bulu, *Bridal Caves,* New Delhi, INTACH, 1995.

Kosambi, D.D., *Myth and Reality,* Bombay, Sangam Press, 1962.

Lewis-Williams, J.D., "Ethnography and Iconography: Aspects of South San Thought and Art", *Man,* 15, 1980, pp. 467-82.

——, *Discovering Southern African Rock Art,* Cape Town, David Philip, 1990.

Mathpal, Yasodhar, "Prehistoric Art of Bhimbetaka, Central India: A Preliminary Study", *JUP,* 41, 1975, pp. 95-107.

Roy, Sarat Chandra, "Some Remains of the Ancient Asuras in the Ranchi District", *JBORS,* 1/2, 1915, pp. 229-253.

Sontheimer, G.D., *Biroba, Maskoba and Khandoba,* Schriftenreihe des Sudasien Institute der Universitat Heidelberg, 120, 1976, Wiesbaden, Fraz Steiner Verlay Gmbtt.

Turner, Victor, *The Forest of Symbols: Aspects of Ndember Ritual,* New York, Ithaca, Cornell University Press, 1967.

Vatsyayan, Kapila, *Traditions of Indian Folk Dance,* New Delhi, Indian Book, 1976.

Wakankar, V.S., "Rock Shelters in Madhya Pradesh", *IAR,* 1957.

3

Boisselier, Jean, *La Statuaire du Champa, EFEO,* LIV, Paris, 1963.

Claeys, Jean-Yves, "Considerations sur la Recherche Archaeologique au Champa et en Indochine", *BEFEO,* LXIV (1947-50), Hanoi. 1951, pp. 89-96.

Groslier, Bernard Philippe, *Indo-China: Art in the Melting Pot of Races,* Germany, Baden-Baden, 1962.

Majumdar, R.C., *Champa: History and Culture of an Indian Colonial Kingdom in the Far East 2nd-16th Century* AD, Book III, Lahore, 1927.

Parmentier, H., *Les Sculptures Chames au Musee de Tourane,* Ars Asiatica, Paris, 1922.

Scoff, Wilfred, *Periplus of the Erythrean Sea: Travel and Trade in the Indian Ocean by a Merchant of the First Century,* London, 1912.

4

Bose, P., *The Indian Colony of Champa,* Madras, 1926.

Claeys, J.Y., "Introduction a letude de L'Annam et du Champa", *BAVH,* Hue, 1934.

Dan Toc Cham, *Luoc Su* (Cham People—A Brief History) in Lau Tu Nhat, 1965.

Dan Toc Hoc, *Cham,* 3, 1994, Ethnographic Studies, Hanoi.

Doanh, Ngo Van, *Thap Cham,* Hanoi, Dan Toc, 1993.

——, *The Culture of Champa,* Hanoi, 1994.

——, *Ancient Towers of Champa,* Hanoi, The Culture Publishing House, 1994.

Dop, Pham Van and Cuong, Nguyen Viet, "Nguoi Cham O Dong Bang Song Cuu Long" (Cham People of Cuu Long River), *Ethnological Issue in the Cuu Long River Delta,* Mac Duong (ed.), Hanoi, Social Sciences Publishing House, 1991.

Fitzgerald, C.P., *The Southern Expansion of the Chinese People: Southern Field and Southern Ocean,* Canberra, 1972.

Phan, Xuan Bien, "Tinh da dang cua van hoc Cham" (The Diversity of Cham Culture), *Social Sciences Journal,* 4, 1990, pp. 74-80.

Pho, Cao Xuan, *Dien Khac* (Cham Sculpture), Hanoi, Social Sciences Publishing House, 1988.

Phuong, Tran Ky, *Mi-sone trong lich Su Nghe Thuat Cham* (Mi-son in the History of Cham Arts), Danang, Danang Publishing House, 1988.

——, *Museum of Cham Sculpture in Da Nang,* Hanoi, Foreign Languages Publishing House, 1987.

Rosson, Philip, *Art of South-East Asia (Cambodia, Vietnam, and Thailand),* Thames Hudson, 1990.

Stern, Philippe, *L'Art du Champa (ancient Annam) et son evolution,* Paris, 1942.

Sivaramamurti, C., *Natraja in Art, Thought and Literature,* New Delhi, Publications Division, Ministry of Information and Broadcasting, Government of India, 1974.

——, *The Art of India,* New York, Hary N. Abrame, 1977.

Tan, Ha Van, "Tu Bau Tro den Sa'Huynh" (From Bau Tro to Sa Huynh), *PHKCH,* 1980, pp. 142-43.

5

Coedés, George, *Indianized States of Southeast Asia,* Singapore, University of Malaysia Press, 1968.

Coomaraswamy, Ananda K., *History of Indian and Indonesian Art*, New York, 1927.

Dupont, Pierre, "Les Apports Chinois dans le Styles Bouddhique de Dong-du'o'ng", *BEFEO,* LXIV (1947-50), Hanoi, 1951, pp. 267-74.

Groslier, Bernard Philippe, *Indo-China: Art in the Melting Pot of Races,* London, Methuen, 1962.

Hall, D.G.E., *A History of South-East Asia,* New York, 1970.

Majumdar, R.C., "The Inscriptions of Champa" in *Champa: History and Culture of an Indian Colonial Kingdom in the Far East 2nd-16th Century* AD, Book III, Delhi, 1985.

Parmentier, H., *Inventaire Descriptif des Monuments Chams de l'Annam,* Paris, 1909.

Rougier, Virgile, "Nouvelles Decouvertes Chams au Quang-nam", *BCAI,* 1912.

Sarkar, H.B., *Cultural Relations between India and South-East Asian Countries*, New Delhi, 1985.

Tarling, Nicholas, *The Cambridge History of South-East Asia (from early time to* c. *1800*), I, Cambridge University Press, 1992.

6

Chhabra, B.C., "Three More Yupa Inscriptions of King Mūlavarman from Koetei (East Borneo)", *JGIS,* XII, 1945.

Coedés, George, "A Propos de la date d'edification d'Angkor Vat", *JA,* January-March, 1920.

——, *Les, Etats Hindouises d'Indochine et d'Indonesie,* Paris, 1948.

Giles, Herbert A., *Chinese-English Dictionary,* I-III, London, Grafton Street, 1912.

Giteau, Madeleine, *Khmer Sculpture and the Angkor Civilization,* London, 1965.

Janse, Olov R.T., *Archaeological Research in Indo-China,* I, Cambridge, Mass, Harvad Yenching Institute, 1947, II, Cambridge, Mass: Harvard Yenching Institute, 1951, III, Bruges: Institute Belge des Hautes Etudes Chinoises.

Karlgern, Bernhard, "The Date of Early Dongson Culture", *BMFEA,* 14, 1942, pp. 1-28.

Majumdar, R.C., *Suvarṇadvipa,* I, Decca, 1937.

Mouhot, Henri, *Diary: Travels in the Central Parts of Siam, Cambodia and Laos During the Years 1858-61.* Abridged and edited by Christopher Pym, London, 1966.

Parmentier, Henri, *L'Art Khmer Primitif,* I, Paris, 1927.

Remusat, G. de Coral, *L'art Khmer,* Paris, 1940.

Solheim II, Wilhelm G., "A Brief History of the Dongson Concept", *AP, XXVIII/1,* 1988-1989, pp. 23-30.

Vogel, Jean Philippe, "The Yupa Inscriptions of King Mūlavarman from Koetei (East Borneo)", *BKI,* 74, 1918, pp. 167-232.

7

Coedés, George, *Angkorian Introduction,* tr. Emily Floyol Gardiner, Singapore, Oxford University Press, 1990.

Cunningham, A., *The Stūpa of Bharhut,* Varanasi, 1962.
Goldstücker, Theodor, *Sanskrit Dictionary,* 1856.
Groslier, Bernard and Arthaud, Jacques, *Angkor: Art and Civilization,* tr. Eric Ernshaw Smith, New York, Frederic A. Preager, 1966.
MacDonald, Malcolm, *Angkor,* London, Jonathan Cape, 1958.
Mani, Vetham, *Puranic Encyclopaedia,* Delhi, 1979.
Parmentier, Henri, *Angkor,* Saigon, Albert Portail, 1950.
Rao, T.A, Gopinath, *Elements of Hindu Iconography,* II, Delhi, 1968.
White, Peter P., "The Temples of Angkor: Ancient Glory in Stone", edited and photographs by Wilbur E. Garrett, *NG,* 161/5, May 1982, pp. 552-89.

8

Dodd, W.C., *Tai Race: Elder Brothers of the Chinese,* compiled and edited by Cedar Rapids, The Torch Press, 1923.
Lebar, Frank M. (ed.), *Laos: Its People, Its Society, Its Culture,* New Haven, 1960.
Miettinien, J.O., *Classical Dance and Theatre of South-East Asia,* Singapore, 1992.
Naenna, Patricia, *Costume and Culture: Vanishing Textiles of Some of the Tai Groups in Laos P.D.R.,* Chiang Mai, Thailand, Studio Naenna Co. Ltd., 1990.
Seidenfaden, Eric, *The Tai Peoples,* Bangkok, The Siam Society, 1958.
Susan, Conway, *Thai Textiles,* London, British Museum Press, 1992.

9

Barth, A., "La Stele de Vat Phu", *BEFEO, II,* 1902, pp. 235-40.
Bhattacharyya, Benoytosh, *The Indian Buddhist Iconography,* Calcutta, 1958.
Coedés, George, *Les Peuples de la Peninsule Indochinoise,* Paris, 1961.
Colani, Madelaine, *Megalithes du Haut Laos: Lua Pantran ninh,* Paris, 1936.
Diskul, Prince M.C. Subhdradis, *Art in Thailand: A Brief History,* 7th edition, Bangkok, 1991.
Dommen, Arthur, J., *Laos: Keystone of Indonesia,* Boulder and London, Westview, 1985.
Dutt, Sukumar, "Laos" in *Buddhism in East Asia,* New Delhi, Indian Council for Cultural Relations, 1966.
Foucher, A., *Etude sur l"Iconographie Buddhique de l'Inde,* Ist partie, Paris, 1900, 2e. partie, 1905.
Frederic, Louis, *The Art of South-East Asia (Temple and Sculpture),* New York, Harry N. Abrams.
Getty, Alice, *The Gods of Northern Buddhism,* 1st edition, Oxford, 1914 and the 2nd edition, Oxford, 1928.
Gozheva, N.A., "Laos" in *Myths and Legends in the Art of the Countries of South-East Asia,* (in Russian), Moscow, 1990, pp. 99-107.
Gozheva, N.A. and Sorokina, "Art of Laos" in *Art of Indo-China,* (in Russian), Moscow, 1991, pp. 38-45.
Groslier, Bernard Philippe, *Indo-China: Art in the Melting Pot of Races,* London, Methuen, 1962.

Guignard, T., "Note Historique et Ethnographique sur le Laos et les Thay", *Revue Indochinoise,* I, 1904.
Helpern, Joel M., *Laos Profile,* Dalley Bk. Service, 1990.
Keyes, Charles, F., *South-east Asian Research Tools: Laos,* Hawaii, University of Hawaii Press, 1979.
Luce, G.H., "The Early Syam in Burma's History", *JSS,* XLVI 2, 1958.
Majumdar, R.C., *Hindu Colonies in the Far East,* Calcutta, 1953.
Parmentier, Henari, *L'Art du Laos, EPFEO,* XXXV, Paris, 1954.
Ratnam, Perala, *Laos and Its Culture,* New Delhi, 1982.
Rawson, Philip, *The Art of South-East Asia,* London, Thames and Hudson, 1990.
Sahai, Sachchidanand, *The Rāmāyaṇa in Laos: A Study in the Gvāy Dvorabhi,* Delhi 1976.
——, *Kṛṣṇa Saga in Laos,* New Delhi, 1978.
——, *The Rāma Jātaka in Laos: A Study in the Phra Lăk Phra Lām,* 2 vols., New Delhi, 1996.
Sarkar, H.B., "Bengal and Her Traffic Routes in the Bay of Bengal and South-East Asia (*c.* 300 BC-AD 300)", *JAS,* XIV/1, 1972, pp. 74-90.
Seckel, Dietrich, *The Art of Buddhism,* London, Methuen, 1964.
Sehgal, S.R., *India and Laos: A Study of Cultural Relations,* New Delhi, 1969.
Terwiel, B.J., *The Tai of Assam and Ancient Tai Ritual,* I, Gaya, Bihar, 1980.
Trenckner, V., *The Milindapanho,* London, Pali Text Society, 1962.
Turner, Jane (ed.), "Laos" in *The Dictionary of Art* (Kettle to Leathart), 18, London, Macmillan Publishers Limited, 1996, pp. 761-777.
Vira, Raghu, "The Literature of Lava" in *India and Asia: A Cultural Symphony,* Delhi, 1978.
Whitaker, Donald P. et al., *Laos: A Country Study,* Foreign Area Studies, Washington, Washington University Press, 1985.

## 10

Bulcke, C., *The Ramakatha,* Allahabad, 1971.
Deydier, H., "Indianistic Researches in Laos", *JOR* XXIV, 1954-55, pp. 9-14.
Nivat, Dhani, "The Rāma Jātaka: A Lao Version of the Story of Rāma", *JSS,* 36.
Raghavan, V., *The Rāmāyaṇa in Greater India,* South Gujarat University, Surat, 1975.
Sahai, Sachchidanand, "Sources of the Lao Rāmāyaṇa", *Indian Horizon,* XXI/1-2, April-July 1972, pp. 70-81.
——, *The Rāmāyaṇa in Laos: A Study in the Gvāy Dvorabhi,* Delhi, 1976.
——, *The Rāma Jātaka in Laos: A Study in the Phra Lăk Phra Lām,* 2 vols., New Delhi, 1996,
Tinh, Vo Thu, "Phra Lăk Lām", *BARL,* 6, 1971, pp. 1-94.

## 11

Baptat, P.V., *2500 Years of Buddhism,* New Delhi, Publications Division, Ministry of Information and Broadcasting, 1971.
Basham, A.L., *The Wonder That was India,* New Delhi, 1967.
Berval, Rene De, *Kingdom of Laos,* Saigon, 1959.

Buribhand, Luand Boribal, *Pravatisat Pra Putasasana Nai Pratethai* (The History of Buddhism in Thailand), Bangkok, Chatra Press, 1955.

Chandra, Lokesh and Ratnam, Perala, "The Rāmāyaṇa in Laos: Vientiane Version", *Studies in Indo-Asian Art and Culture,* 5, Commemorative Volume on the 75th Birthday of Acharya Raghuvira, New Delhi, 1977, pp. 183-216.

Deydier, Henri, "The Rāmāyaṇa in Laos", *JRAS,* 22.

——, "Les Origines et la Naissance de Ravana dans le Rāmāyaṇa Laotien", *BEFEO,* LXIX (1947-50), Hanoi, 1951, pp. 141-46.

Garnier, F., *Voyage d'exploration in Indochine,* Paris, 1901.

Groslier, Bernard Philippe, *Indo-China: Art in the Melting Pot of Races,* London, Meththen, 1962.

Jermsawtdi, Promsak, *Thai Art with Indian Influences,* New Delhi, Abhinav Publications, 1979.

Lafont, P.B., *P'a·Lăk P'a Lām, EFEO,* 6, 1957.

"Laos", Microsoft Encarta 97 Encyclopaedia, Microsoft Corporation, 1993-96.

Lyons, Elizabeth, *Arts of Bangkok Period,* Bangkok, 1968.

Marchal, H., "L'Art decoratif au Laos", *AA,* X/2, 1962.

Monavitoon, Saeng, *Sasanawongsa* (History of Religion), Bangkok, 1963.

Parmentier, H., *L'Art due Laos, Publications, EFEO,* XXXV, Paris, 1954, revised 1988.

Ratnam, Perala, *Laos and its Culture,* New Delhi, Tulsi Publishing House, 1982.

Sahai, Sachchidanand, *Rāmāyaṇa in Laos: A Study in the Gvāy Dvorabhi,* Delhi, B.R. Publishing House, 1979.

Siridham, *Karnapoklaong Kanasong nai Yukboran thuang Yukpatchuban,* pak I (The Administration of Buddhist Saṅgha from Ancient to Present Times, Part I), Yungli Press, Bangkok, 1933.

Souk, T. Boun, *L'Image du Bouddha dans l'art Lao,* Vientiane, 1971.

Tinh, Vo Thu, "Phra Lăk Phra Lām", *BARL,* 6, 1971, pp. 1-94.

Turner, Jane (ed.), *The Dictionary of Art* (Kettle to Leathart), 18, London, Macmillan Publishers Limited, 1996, pp. 761-77.

Yupho, Dhanti, *Suvarṇabhūmi,* Bangkok, 1967.

# Contributors

**Induja Awasthi**

Retired Reader, Miranda House, University of Delhi, Induja Awasthi a well-known linguist and art critic, has travelled extensively in different countries of South-East Asia. She has written a number of research papers on different versions of the Rāmāyaṇa in India and South-East Asia. She has also participated in the national and international seminars and conferences in India and abroad.

**D.K. Bhattacharya**

Former Professor, Department of Anthropology, University of Delhi, is an eminent anthropologist and archaeologist. He has travelled widely in India and discovered Paleolithic tools from various regions. He has published several research papers and books on Paleolithic tools and techniques. He has organised and participated in various national and international conferences.

**Lokesh Chandra**

Director, International Academy of Indian Culture, New Delhi, a well-known indologist, has multi-disciplinary approach in his research work. He is the author of numerous research papers and books including *New Tibeto-Mongol Pantheon*, 20 volumes; *Sanskrit Texts from the Imperial Palace at Peking*, 22 volumes; *The Esoteric Iconography of Japanese Mandalas; Tibetan-Sanskrit Dictionary*, 2 volumes and *Thousand Armed Avalokiteśvara.*

**A.K. Das**

Former Professor and Head, Department of Museology, National Museum Institute of History of Art, Conservation and Museology

(Deemed to be a University), National Museum, New Delhi has wide experience of research and teaching. At present he is Director, Lal Bahadur Sastri Museum, New Delhi. He is also a member of the International Committee for Museums and Ethology.

**M.N. Deshpande**

Former Director-General, Archaeological Survey of India, an eminent archaeologist and art historian, has excavated various prehistoric sites of India. He has served as a Visiting Professor and Fellow of Allahabad University, Allahabad; Advisor; Nehru Centre, Mumbai for the Discovery of India Project and Aditi Exhibition in the Festival of India, USA. He has published a number of research papers and books.

**Bachchan Kumar**

In charge of South-East Asian Studies, Indira Gandhi National Centre for the Arts, New Delhi, is an art-historian. He has published several research papers on art and culture of South-East Asia in the learned journals. Besides, he has participated at the national and international conferences in India and abroad. He is the author of a number of books including *The Bhils: An Ethno Historic Analysis* and has edited a monograph entitled *Glimpses of Early Indo-Indonesian Culture: Collected Papers of Himansu Bhusan Sarkar.* He is the recipient of Indian Archaeological Society Award, 2002, New Delhi and Asia Fellows Awards 2004 & 2007, Bangkok, Thailand.

**Neeru Misra**

Senior Director, Indian Council for Cultural Relations, New Delhi, is an eminent art historian. She has travelled widely in the different countries of South-East Asia and made in-depth study on Angkor Wat in Cambodia and Rāmāyaṇa reliefs at the different monasteries of Laos and Thailand. Based on her experiences, she has written a number of research papers. She has also written a book on medieval India.

**Himanshu Prabha Ray**

Associate Professor, Jawaharlal Nehru University, New Delhi, has travelled extensively in Indonesia, Malaysia, Singapore and Thailand, for her research projects under Homi Bhabha Fellowship. She was a visiting fellow at the Cornell University, Ithaca, USA. She has published a number of research papers and books including *Monastery and Guild: Commerce Under the Satavahanas* and *Colonial Archaeology in South Asia (1944-1948): The Legacy of Sir Mortimer Wheeler in India.*

**J.C. Sharma**

Former Secretary, Ministry of External Affairs, Government of India, New Delhi, is a well-known art historian. He was the Indian Ambassador to Vietnam. During his posting in Vietnam, he did extensive survey of the Cham temples in Vietnam. He has written a number of research papers on Champa and published a book entitled *Hindu Temples in Vietnam.*

**K.M. Srivastava**

Former Director, Archaeological Survey of India, an eminent archaeologist, has excavated various archaeological sites in India and abroad. The most outstanding discovery made by him was the identification of the town of Kapilvastu at Piprahwa. He has published a number of research papers and books including *Angkor Wat and Cultural Ties with India* and *Apsarās at Angkor Wat.*

# Index